An Adventure In After-Death Communication

Conversations
with Tom

Walda Woods

White Rose Publishing
N. Andover, MA

Conversations with Tom: An Adventure In After-Death Communication
by Walda Woods

Copyright © 2000 Walda Woods

Hardcopy Edition published 2001 by White Rose Publishing

ISBN 0-9706100-3-3

Published by:

White Rose Publishing

120 Kingston Street,
North Andover, MA 01845
Phone: (978) 686-0491
Fax: (978) 681-9382
Email: Noel95@aol.com

To order additional copies by credit card, call toll-free:

1-888-281-5170

Manufactured in the United States of America

Contents

Dedication

To Tom, my soul-mate in Heaven

"If you knew what death was really like,
you would never call it death...."

— Tom Woods
July, 1999

Foreword by Patricia Mischell

How wonderful this book is! Written with such a rare, tender and thorough perception of what a woman feels and experiences after the death of her husband, I know it will comfort and inspire a world so much in need of its message.

As each individual life unfolds, it brings with it joy and happiness as well as grief, suffering, feelings of hopelessness, and a need to find answers to the mysteries of life and death. I believe this book offers some of the answers we all seek and a message of hope.

As a child, I had a near-death-experience, a brief adventure I found overwhelmingly pleasant. That life-altering experience led me to recognize certain abilities within myself and learn how to use them to penetrate the veil separating our world from the world of the afterlife. Over the years I have learned to speak with those who have already crossed the barrier between our worlds. I have brought back messages to share with those who needed to hear that their loved ones were happy. That same need brought the author of this book to me.

Walda contacted me after seeing me on a national television show. She was looking for some kind of closure and understanding as to why her husband had passed away so quickly.

Through Walda's many conversations with her husband, she learned as so many others had, that he continues to live spiritually, even though his physical life had ended. I believe her husband had a message he wanted to share with us about his survival and his continuing love for those he had left behind. Furthermore, he knew his message would bring healing to the thousands who would read it.

While reading this book, I thanked God for the courage of this woman to bring her message to others. I hope that it may ease the suffering and pain they feel from the loss of a loved one.

The author and I have become friends during the many months she has been writing this book. I consider the material accurate and believe this book was long-planned and carefully developed between her and her husband on a very deep spiritual level even before he left this earth.

Although grieving his death, she has marshaled her emotion into a positive force. In this book, she has bared her soul in her search to answer the questions that haunt each of us—the never-ending whys. I believe Walda has answered them in this book and so will you.

— Patricia Mischell
Author of *Beyond Positive Thinking*

Preface by Tom Woods

Welcome to the world of Spirit! There is a celebration in Heaven every time someone picks up this book. As we enter the new millennium, mankind is becoming aware of a new spirituality, a higher consciousness necessary to bring peace to an angry world. This book is one of many resources that will assist you in your enlightenment process and we have tried to fill the pages with love and inspiration.

We, here in my world, realize that death is not easy for you to discuss. What we have found, however, is that your interest peaks when the loss of a loved one occurs. Or when someone close to you is dying. Faith and love become shrouded with fear and doubt. The result is confusion and anger. It is then that you begin to look for answers.

My wonderful wife and I decided to work together on this project as a gift of love to all of you who are seeking those answers. She has taken many risks in order to do this and I applaud her courage. Doing spiritual work in a physical world is sometimes discouraging and I am quite aware that there were times when she wanted to quit. But her strong commitment to purpose gave her the momentum to keep going.

Together we have reached the highest level of understanding between our two dimensions of existence. The connection that we continue to share must act as a reminder to all who read this that love never dies.

It is important to understand that you are so much more than your physical body. The soul and spirit—the very essence of who you are—continue on to a new dimension of Light, Love and God Consciousness. Death is just moving from one room to another. It's like going home after a long separation. Please know that you will see your loved ones once again when it is your time to cross the bridge. Until then, you have work to do. Live with the highest intentions, give love to others and have faith in the power of Spirit and God.

I am not dead. I have only come home.

What Is Dying?

A ship sails and I stand—watching til she
fades on the horizon and someone
at my side says, "She is gone."

Gone where? Gone from my sight, that is all;
she is just as large as when I saw her. The
diminished size and total loss of sight is in
me, not in her, and just at the moment
when someone at my side says, "She is gone,"
there are others who are watching her coming,
and the other voices take up a glad shout,
 "There she comes!"— and that is dying.

— Bishop Brent

A Tribute to Tom

Tom was the love of my life. He swept me off my feet and took my breath away for thirty earth years. He was my best friend and confidant, and never in that span of time did I feel I couldn't share absolutely everything with this man. My heart and soul were his. And to him, I was the sexiest, smartest, funniest and most compassionate person in the world. He loved me when I was fat, skinny, employed and unemployed. He loved me when I was having a bad day as well as when the world was my oyster. We were bonded together with a burning love that I am so very grateful to have experienced.

When he died he left a tremendous legacy of caring and love. Over seven hundred people paid their respects to a man who had touched their lives in some way. He had such an excitement and love for life that his effect on people was extraordinarily positive. Our good friend Kathy describes Tom as an "energy" who would walk into a room and suddenly transform everyone with his humor and compassionate presence.

Tom had an emotional childhood. Growing up in a family of nine children would have been challenge enough. But at the age of eleven, his beloved mother Ruth died of cancer. Traumatic as this must have been, the family vowed to remain close, leaning on each other while trying to maintain a positive outlook. As a teenager, Tom was not interested in school or his future. He managed to become a troubled delinquent with a very large chip on his shoulder. Luckily, by the time he turned eighteen, he had decided that there must be a better way out of the poverty and hopelessness. He set out to find it, and by the time we were married almost two years later, Tom had a clear vision of his future and the goals necessary to make it happen.

I'm not quite sure what transformed him into the caring, thoughtful individual he became. I suspect that he may somehow have had a glimpse of his soul's purpose—"Touched by the Divine", as some may say. And through that brief encounter, he succeeded in setting himself back on course. He was never outwardly religious, but he managed to maintain a vague belief in a Universal Intelligence. His desire to know God was discreet yet intense, but was rarely a topic of conversation between us. I think this may have been because we differed in our perceptions of what the Divine Source actually represented. To me, God was an all-encompassing, loving, universal energy. To Tom, God was an angry, punishing and judgmental being. I pictured the Divine as being a part of me. He pictured it as an entity outside of himself. Tom believed in an afterlife but was unsure of what it comprised. He was fascinated by the Near Death Experience but limited his interest to an occasional PBS special. I had begun reading about life after death, and would describe to him some of the more exciting details. I was hoping to eliminate his natural fear of death, just as I had already done for myself. My feelings are that before he died, he was at the "I'll believe it when I see it" stage.

Like most of us, Tom had his faults. He was not always as tolerant as he should have been. And he had a habit of either "tuning out" or arguing against opinions which did not coincide with his. He wore his human traits innocently but his intentions were always filled with light.

A member of the International Brotherhood of Teamsters for many years, he was always a jeans, flannel shirt and workboots kind of guy. He took pleasure in all spectator sports, spending many a Saturday afternoon at the local pub with his friends watching a game on wide-screen. (I used to tease him by saying that he would probably drop a wager on two ants walking across the floor.) He loved his new Chevy Blazer, the ocean, our cats Ben and Jerry, fireworks and any excuse to get together with friends and family.

As far as education was concerned, he courageously passed his high-school equivalency exam at the age of forty-one. And during the years we were together he supplemented his knowledge by reading and studying on his own. He knew a little bit about every subject imaginable and was a whiz at current events and politics.

He had a smile that would light up my soul, a laugh that was remarkably contagious and a gentleness that melted my heart.

This was Tom.

Author's Note

This book contains material that may be contrary to the teachings of some religions. It is indeed my story, however, and its purpose is for healing, not to sway anyone either way in terms of religious beliefs.

At this time I feel it appropriate to mention that my son Tommy recently converted to Catholicism and is a devoutly serious communicant. As much as he loves me and understands my passion for the work I do, he has chosen to remain constant in his loyalty to the beliefs and teachings of the Roman Catholic Church.

For this I applaud him—in having the courage to stand on conviction while at the same time remaining a constant source of love and gentleness in my life.

Acknowledgments

I believe that God and the universe send us the people we need to help us through tragedy. For me there have been many and I will attempt to thank most of them here.

I would first like to mention the team who helped with the resuscitation attempts on Tom: Jane Chase, Cindi Lanoue, Kirsten McDevitt, Ron Heggarty and the North Andover Fire Department Paramedics. You gave me a gift too precious to comprehend. Because of your efforts, I had a few more hours with Tom before he died, and for this, my dear friends, I will be forever grateful.

To Kathy and Bob for your never-ending love and patience. Thank you, Kathy, for the wonderful pictures of Tom that I shall always treasure. And Bob, I will always be grateful for your kindness in driving me to the hospital that night and never complaining when I cried on your shoulder.

To Audrey and Frank, my constant support system; for being there and understanding my needs no matter how outrageous they may have seemed.

To Charlene and Bill, for keeping things under control during the most frightening time of my life.

To Julie O'Brien for all of your prayers, compassion and help during a time when I kept asking why.

To Irene Sher for your continued love and wisdom and all the hugs I so badly needed.

To Kevin and Celeste for your warmth and sympathy. The expressions on your faces said it all.

To Cath Cavanaugh and Louise Donahue, the two friends who never forgot me or the pain I was in. You kept me busy and touched my heart.

To Bob and Cindi, and their boys Mark and Craig, for caring so much and being there for my family.

And to all of our many friends who came to my rescue with phone calls and visits and allowed me to talk about this as much as I needed to.

To Patricia Mischell, "my soul sister", who has taken time from her busy schedule to help me to learn more about life after death. She has become monumental in this part of my journey. Communication with Tom has helped me to heal and her unselfish guidance and direction continue to comfort me.

Heartfelt thanks to Judy Guggenheim for her gracious assistance and support when I needed it most.

And a great big hug and thanks to Tony Stubbs, my editor and agent, who went above and beyond to help a very anxious Lightseeker.

To my mother, Myda, who had to watch me go through this pain, who always knew just the right words and who cried right along with me. May she and Tom have many Irish and Armenian dinners together in the afterlife.

To my sister, Myda Jr., and her husband Mel, for all their sacrifices and for the love and comfort they gave me even though their own lives were in turmoil.

To my nephew Jason, who has had to bear losing three very close people in his life in the span of two years. Thank you for having that wonderful ingredient that makes me smile, and for not giving up when the house seemed so empty. Thank you too, for your strength and success in overcoming this tragedy.

To my father, Walter. While he lay dying, he taught me the true meaning of forgiveness and unconditional love.

And to Tommy, Jr., the brightest light in my life. You had to be strong at a time when you needed to weep. You held me up as I tried to console you. Thank you for being such a tremendous source of love and gentleness in my life.

And to all extended family members, a gracious thank you for your love and kindness.

I must extend my gratitude also to Tom's family, for their unconditional comfort and love. To his sisters, brothers and their families as follows: Marsha and Junior Pierce, Karen and Michael Woods, Kate and Dick Roberts, Ruth Anne and Tony Lucci, Val and Buddy Woods, Danny and Nancy Woods, Bill Woods and Jack Woods.

To Patrick and Karen Woods, whose compassion filled all the gaps.

A loving thank you to my nephew Michael Woods who has continued to keep Tom's memory alive with the annual golf tournaments.

A special thank you to my angel-guides who have helped prepare me for this mission of grief. Their guidance continues to assist me every day.

And finally, to the Divine Source, which is God—the discovery of my divine heritage has given me the wisdom needed for this great journey.

Introduction

Death is simply a shedding of the physical body like the butterfly shedding its cocoon. It is a transition to a higher state of consciousness where you continue to perceive, to understand, to laugh, and grow.

— Elisabeth Kubler-Ross, M.D.

Western cultures, supposedly civilized, do not know how to deal with death, the dying process or grief. We don't want to talk about it or even recognize it. Some years ago, as part of the training curriculum for a financial career, I sold life insurance and was amazed at how many people just didn't want to acknowledge the inevitable. ("I'm young. I'm healthy. I have too much to do. I'm not going to die.")

We start dying on the day we're born. We are all dying. We are all terminal. Of course, we should care for our bodies, but no one on this planet can be guaranteed even one more second of this fragile thing we call life.

As for the doctors, when I tried to discuss my mother's prognosis and the inevitability of her death, I was dismayed at how they became squeamish, unable to look me in the eye or bring themselves to even use the word "death." I needed to know the worst-case scenario, yet all they could do was beat around the bush.

So why are we so afraid? And why don't we make death and dying a part of our life study? Many cultures do, going so far as to teach it in religion classes, schools and the home. If only we knew what to expect from death and the afterlife, and accepted it as an integral part of life, then we would all live more fulfilling lives, joyful lives, compassionate and loving lives where nothing is taken for granted. And at the hour of death, no fear, no doubt, no resistance, but just a joyous acceptance of the transition about to be made.

In the spiritual sense, there would be more *understanding* of life itself, why we are here, what we need to do to complete this leg of the journey, and how to prepare for the next. Life is a serious mission and we don't have a clue how to make the most out of it.

Western cultures don't know how to grieve. Many researchers have studied the grief process, and identified the many stages of grief, and the many styles of grieving. But as long as we view death as only a *loss*, we will be stymied as to how face it. Of course, no matter how "spiritual" we become, we will experience loss, and there are no shortcuts to dealing with grief. But most of us do not know how to approach a grieving person. People mean well, but are *afraid* of grief. They don't know how to deal with you.

In my workshops, I teach that if you feel like crying, then cry. If you feel like looking at pictures or going through memories of the deceased, do it. If you feel like talking about your loved one, then find someone who will listen and just talk, talk, talk. This is your bowl of cherries, so stir it up any way you want, as long as you're not doing anything illegal, immoral or unsafe. The key is to get beyond the "loss" phase so that you can once again become a useful member of the human (spiritual) race.

The loss of loved ones through death is only a temporary, physical loss. You will be reunited with them someday, but right now you have work to do here. Now, detachment is hard. With Tom, I was so swept up in the detachment part that I forgot about the other detachments I'd had so far. Life is full of them. We fear detachment because it means letting something go. Unprepared and unaware of how to cope, disconnection looks like the enemy. "Woe is me. I hurt. I no longer have 'that person' in my life."

What is easy to forget is that when we lose something, we have the innate ability to gain something else! When one door closes, another opens. Sometimes, what we gain may be intangible, such as a lesson learned, or a sense of independence. So, embrace this lesson, explore your new freedom, and be thankful for it. It's fuel for the long trip ahead.

Other times, the payoff is a direct betterment of ourselves and how we view what's happened. When you marry, you give up the single life, but gain the wonderful companionship and love shared by two people in union. When you have a child, you give up most of your freedom to come and go as a couple, but your life is enriched by the chance to love and nurture as only a parent can. Losing your job can be devastating— take it from one who knows—but it freed me up to make new things happen and I did. I ended up in a job that was infinitely more fulfilling than the one I lost, and never looked back. Divorce, one of the ultimate detachments, can be devastating for a woman, but the prize is renewed independence, and the chance to become successful despite the fact that she thought her life was over.

Rabbi Earl Grollman said it best: "Grief is a process. Recovery is a choice." We all have the tools to make our lives wonderful. Each one of us has these gifts, but we may expect everything to just drop out of the sky into our laps. Boom. "I'm well again." We must realize that there is a certain amount of work involved or we wouldn't be here. The reward is not what you acquire, but *the accomplishment of reaching your goal.*

So in viewing your situation after a loved one dies, you must have the knowing, the believing, and the desire to take your situation that giant step further. Detaching from a loved one following death is tough, and it's healthy to see it as such. But you must not allow your perceived loss to govern your life. Your existence here is precious and you are absolutely essential to the unfolding of God's universal plan.

After Tom's death, I was overwhelmed by an inner calling to research and study death and dying. The grief that I experienced was all consuming, and my only way out seemed to be to learn about the afterlife— where he was, what he encountered during the transition, and how I could connect with him. He had already begun to send signs, and I could feel his thoughts pouring through my mind. I had no idea how to analyze what was happening, but I knew that something was indeed happening! The energy that filled my home was so peaceful but at the same time charged with electrical intensity. I knew my expedition into the unknown would be thrilling but I had no idea that I would end up where I am now.

Angels and Guides

I became more and more aware of the divine/angelic guidance in my life. My direction in life was unfolding in a series of dynamic events and I could no longer deny the existence of the spiritual assistance I was receiving. As an example, let me introduce my own inspiring entourage of angels and guides, and show how each interacts with me daily. I'm sure that many more will make their presence known to me as my life unfolds.

Noel is my spiritual angel. A gentle and loving teacher who has been with me for many lifetimes, he is a master teacher who has only my soul's purpose and balance at heart. His many teachings include meditation, channeling, healing, and forgiveness. An extremely powerful entity, he helps me strive for the perfection I need to fulfill my purpose.

Nora is my writing angel. She appeared when I began writing my first book. Always graceful with her words, she guides me to do my best work. She is the producer, if you will, who decides the format of everything I write, including my lectures and seminars. Nora loves nature, and the first time I met her, she was standing near some mountains with the breeze blowing through her hair. She gently nudges me when I start to get lazy with my work and makes sure that I wake up each morning much earlier than I'd like to.

David is my "connecting" angel, in that he keeps my connection with my deceased husband Tom as strong as it can be. David is very laid back and easy to talk to. He makes sure Tom and I stay connected, while at the same time accomplishing what we need to do in our separate worlds. David brought the two of us together after Tom passed and showed me what I needed to do to be able to make the "dialogue" clear enough to dissect and understand it.

White Eagle is my spirit guide for health. A wise Native American spirit guide, he works with herbal and holistic healing treatments. His major theme is the mind/body/spirit balance. While he is strict when it comes to my health, he never scolds or is angered when I fail to follow his directions. However, when I see a feather on the ground, it's his way of reminding me to get back on track.

Bernard is my financial guide, here to help me handle the immense financial risk I've had to take while pursuing these new frontiers. He has shown me how to take a dollar and stretch it to its limit, and "jabs" me when I get too extravagant. His synchronistic signs always lead me to the cheapest airfares and other worthwhile bargains!

Sergio is my spirit guide for fun and relaxation. He is beautifully dressed, complete with silk shirt and lots of flashy jewelry. He is dark complected, and has a foreign accent, at least, his thoughts come through that way. Sergio nudges me when I am working too hard and need a break. He keeps my social calendar busy and loves to be around people, but is also happy when I relax with a good book or an inspiring movie.

Luke is my business guide, and the newest addition to the group. Because the publication of my first book was not advancing, he stepped forward to get me back on track. Suddenly, I had a new agent and progress was finally beginning to happen. Despite his aloof and reserved demeanor, he still emits the most powerful love energy.

The Near Death Experience

I became fascinated with the Near Death Experience (NDE). Drs. Raymond Moody, Melvin Morse, Kenneth Ring and Elisabeth Kubler-Ross, all pioneers in NDE research, have collected extensive data from the millions of people who have claimed to have had an NDE, including one or two among themselves. They have each risked their careers and professional reputations by becoming involved in what many regard as "nonsense." Unfortunately, scientists have decided to dismiss what cannot be "proven" in the laboratory rather than take a giant step forward in what could be the biggest breakthrough in mankind's history.

Serious NDE research started back in the 1970s when the medical community's resuscitation techniques allowed people pronounced clinically dead to be brought back to life, only to recount amazing stories of an afterlife. As well-respected professionals began to publish their work, millions of readers experienced a sense of relief, because having had an NDE themselves, they had been branded certifiably crazy by their doctors, family and friends.

Although NDEs still carry a minor stigma, opinions vary widely and the growing support in this field has finally become apparent. Approximately ten million people have undergone the journey of near death and they report remarkably similar experiences: the tunnel, the light, meeting deceased loved ones and being out-of-body, to name just a few. But the most significant aspect is that most of those returning say that the experience of other dimensions and levels of consciousness profoundly changed their lives. They have a renewed sense of life and spirit, and some are even heightened psychically.

Although most scientists dismiss all this out-of-hand with the theory that these are hallucinations caused by the brain shutting down or various drug-induced states, serious researchers say "not so." The NDE is not like any hallucination or dream known in the scientific arena. The encounter is logical and coherent, and far more intense than any "dream." In dreams, we do not see our own bodies from a detached viewpoint, as is characteristic of an NDE. And if the experience were born of so-called "wishful thinking," material ambitions would probably be part of it, yet these things don't even enter into the experience. Instead, it is usually intensely spiritual, with some form of advice being given by one or more wise counselors.

Open-minded scientists will admit, however, that they have no real explanation for the out-of-body state that most report. In many cases, conversations and events that experiencers say they overheard happened miles from where their body was. Prior beliefs held by experiencers are also not a factor, since believers as well as atheists have NDEs. The most penetrating and convincing accounts are from those with no vested interest in fabrication—children. Dr. Melvin Morse's "Closer to The Light," a book dedicated to the NDEs of children, will convert even the most hardened skeptic.

After-Death Communication

After Death Communication (ADC) occurs more often than people are willing to admit. The fear of being ostracized prevents many people from reporting some of the paranormal happenings after a loved one dies. Of the many books now published on this subject, probably the most informative is *Hello From Heaven* by Bill and Judy Guggenheim. Gentle yet to the point, it offers an excellent introduction and insights into ADC. For example, the authors define ADC as: "A spiritual experience that occurs when someone is contacted directly and spontaneously by a deceased family member or friend."

A startling fifty million Americans have had one or more ADCs, yet most are reluctant to come forward and talk about it. However, many other cultures on the planet, especially aboriginal, openly accept and embrace ADC as a normal part of life, and experiences are freely shared with others. Sadly, Western society insists upon labeling these people as having overactive, grieving imaginations.

ADC contacts can take on many forms:

- Feeling a presence
- Vision of the loved one
- Hearing a voice
- Feeling a touch
- Sense of smell experience
- Symbols and signs
- Synchronistic events
- Dreams of the deceased
- The presence of certain birds and animals
- Electrical events—lights, telephone, TV, radio, clocks, etc.

While researching for their book, the Guggenheims found "that almost all of the experiencers, including some who had been devout skeptics, were transformed emotionally and spiritually by their ADC." As with the NDE, ADC doesn't seem to single out any specific group of people to experience these episodes. From all walks of life and all ages, believers and skeptics alike say that their experiences have helped them to heal from the loss of a loved one.

Discussing ADC in a supportive environment is critical to one's grief work. My seminars and support groups, amidst the tears and memories, are based on an open desire to heal the heart, and sharing ADC experiences always brings joy and transformation. We also practice meditation and discuss the afterlife in depth. Participants leave with a new awareness of knowing and believing that love is eternal and is the one thing that keeps us all connected to the spirit world.

It is important to incorporate Spirit in group activity. After Tom passed, I attended a self-help grief work group, but after seven weeks of rehashing the same old emotional baggage, I found that having no spiritual base from which to draw was wearing me down.

Mediums and Séances

Initially, I was skeptical of mediums who claim to be able to put you in touch with loved ones, at least until I started my own research. Through my growing library of books, I became aware of a whole new field of players: Edgar Cayce, Ruth Montgomery, George Anderson, James Van Praagh and Patricia Mischell are some of the most highly recognized psychic mediums of this century.

Now, all mediums are psychics but psychics are *not* necessarily mediums. A medium has direct communication with other dimensions and can actually see or sense the presence of Spirit. Mediumship has been around since Biblical times and, unfortunately, its popularity has waxed and waned through the centuries. Because of a few well-publicized frauds, many people dismiss this gift as a hoax, and some say it is the work of the devil. The once popular and fashionable Ouija Board, for example, attracts much criticism nowadays. Yes, there *are* dark forces in the lower levels of the other world that will try to influence those who are just out for the sport of it, and many inexperienced people have innocently invited this kind of trouble, so the novice is well-advised to stay away from such devices.

Since I was first thrust into this arena, I have seen many people who have spent years grieving the death of a loved one, only to start healing after just one session with a gifted medium. The reading usually involves specific names and circumstances that the medium could have no way of knowing, even with the most thorough research. And most clients confirm that the deceased show themselves as having the same personality they had while living in the earth. An essence of sorts comes through in the reading, leaving no doubt that the medium is, in fact, in contact with the deceased. We will go into this in more detail in Part One, which describes my own experiences with psychic medium Patricia Mischell.

As the weeks wore on, I read more about the subject of life after death. I was convinced that Tom was definitely communicating with me, but I wasn't sure what he was trying to tell me beyond the fact that he was still around. Sometimes, his thoughts would rush through my head and I soon realized that our minds were somehow "blending" into one. I wanted more. I wanted words and thoughts and concepts. I wanted a two-way conversation but had not the slightest idea of how to go about achieving that.

Little did I know I was gearing up for the ride of my life.

Part One: Tragedy Strikes

Chapter 1

The Man Who Took My Breath Away

It had been such an ordinary day. It was Labor Day weekend and we'd woken up looking forward to our neighborhood's eighteenth annual end-of-summer cookout. "I hope the weather's nice today," I said, sitting up in bed.

Tom yawned. "Supposed to be."

"I hope I have enough food," I said, rummaging through a drawer for a shorts outfit.

Tom came up behind me and wrapped his arms around me. "Walda, stop worrying. You always make enough food to feed an army and if anyone walks away hungry, it's their own fault. And everyone always has a good time. How many years have we been doing these cookouts? Eighteen? And promise me you won't hide every time Kathy tries to take your picture today."

I laughed. "Come on, Tom. You know I don't take good pictures."

"I'm serious. Every time she tries to pop a picture of you, you hide."

I turned in his embrace. "I guess I'm just camera-shy."

He kissed me on the nose.

"So how did you sleep last night?" I asked.

"Not too well." He walked into the bathroom and draped a towel over his shoulder. "My mind just wouldn't shut down. I woke up sweating like I had a bad dream or something. Maybe a nice hot shower will relax me."

Puzzled, I asked, "Are you feeling all right?"

"Yeah, fine. After taking Tommy back to school yesterday, I was just thinking a lot about him. Kids sure do grow up fast."

"I know what you mean. It seems like only yesterday that he was born, and now he's twenty-four and a graduate student. You know, you

1

must have loaded a hundred heavy boxes onto and off that van. And then you drove all the way home in one day. I went to the kitchen to make breakfast, and Tom joined me just as the coffee was ready. He seemed quieter than usual but I figured he was just tired because of his lack of sleep. "Why don't you rest for a while?" I suggested.

As Tom finished his bowl of cereal, he said, "No, I think I'll go to the gym and work out for a little while. That'll make me feel better. When I come home, I'll help you get ready for the party." He kissed me and grabbed his workout bag on the way out.

When Tom came home about an hour later, he pitched right in and began setting up tables, chairs, grills and anything else that needed to be done. "Tom, could you put that table over there instead?"

He gave me an irritated look and said, "Sure," as he turned his back on me.

That's odd, I thought. That's not like him. "Are you sure you're feeling all right?"

"Walda, I'm fine," he snapped, but his abruptness, attitude and walk all made me doubt that everything was fine. With growing concern, I asked, "Would you like me to cook today?"

He looked at me as if I'd suddenly grown antlers or something. "You never cook on the grill. I'm all right. I'll cook."

Before I could ask any further questions, the first of our guests arrived, and side-by-side, Tom and I greeted them, shaking hands and hugging. But as I watched Tom, he seemed to be holding back, not laughing quite as much or quite as loud as usual.

One of the neighborhood children ran past and bumped into him. Usually, he would have laughed it off and made a joke, but today, he turned and said, "Hey, watch where you're going."

This wasn't the Tom I knew. During a quiet moment, I tugged at his sleeve and asked again. "Hey, babe, you feeling okay?"

"Walda, I told you before I'm fine." He rubbed his chest, took a deep breath, and softened his voice. "I'm just tired. Really. That's all."

"Tom, look, we've had a tough couple of days here, what with moving Tommy back to school and this party. How about if I do the cooking today?"

To my amazement, he nodded and handed me the spatula. After thirty years, he was still a very special man and I felt truly blessed to have him in my life, the passion, the humor, the joy that were all part of him. The way he moved, the way he tilted his head when he listened to someone. But somewhere deep inside me, a nagging feeling told me something was very wrong and I was powerless to do anything about it. An awful sense of dread closed in on me like a silent, invisible enemy you know is there but remains hidden in the shadows, so you have no weapons against it.

"How you doing, Babe?" I asked as I grabbed the ketchup from the counter.

"I don't know." He made a face as though he were in pain. "Walda, I feel awfully strange. I feel like I pulled a muscle in my chest. It feels very heavy in my chest."

My own heart froze as I thought of the possibility of something being wrong with his. "Tom, do you want to go to the hospital?"

He shook his head and waved his hands for emphasis. "No, no. I just pulled a muscle. It just feels weird. I'll go downstairs and rest for a while. And don't tell anyone I don't feel well." He was very adamant about that, but somehow I knew that might not be the best thing.

Not long after that, I felt a familiar presence settle into the chair beside me.

"You feeling okay?" I asked Tom as I turned to him.

"Much better, thanks. You got any food left for me?" he asked with a smile.

I playfully nudged his elbow with mine. "I think I can scrounge something up for you, sailor." I went to the food table and brought back a plate piled with a hamburger, sausage, potato salad, baked beans, and a salad. "There's more over there if you want. I just couldn't fit it all on the plate," I said as I handed it to him.

"Thanks, Walda," he said as he gently took the plate from my hands. "This looks great," and he began to eat. As he went back for more, I relaxed, thinking that no one who was sick would have such a hearty appetite.

Tom enjoyed food. He loved everything about it, from shopping for it, to cooking it, to eating it. He was a much better cook than I and he took such pleasure in creating exotic dishes for me to try. Today, he was in his glory, surrounded by friends, laughing, talking and making sure everyone had enough to eat. Then some of the kids caught his attention.

"Mr. Woods! Mr. Woods! Come on and play some ball with us."

He finished the last of his food and joined them in a game. After nine innings of dropped balls, unsuccessful tag-out attempts (he always made it look like the kids won fair and square), and terrible strikeouts, he went back to the food table and ate some more. The music from the boom box mixed with voices and laughter carried the sounds of friendship into the evening.

I watched Tom through the crowd and noticed that while he ate and visited and laughed, something still didn't seem quite right. He seemed on edge and a couple of times I saw his hands tighten into fists as though trying to contain his temper or block out pain. This was so unlike him that my relaxed mood began to wane.

"Walda, there must a hundred people here," he remarked. I will never forget the grin that spread across his face. He loved people and loved being with them. "Look at all these people. We have to get pictures of this. Walda, try to get lots of pictures. This is great. This is the biggest crowd we've ever had."

I reached for the camera, pointed, and tried to snap the shot, but nothing happened. Abruptly his mood changed.

"What's the matter with you? Can't you even take a simple picture?" I saw his hand move to his chest.

Shocked, I looked at him in disbelief. In all our years together, he had rarely raised his voice to me, much less spoken to me in exasperation like that. "It's okay, Tom," I said, trying to calm him. "It probably just needs some new batteries. I'll go get some."

"No, no. You're probably at the end of the roll. You need new film," he said irritably.

"Fine. I have more film. No problem." I reached into my pocket and put a new roll of film in. However, instead of pressing the advance button, I inadvertently pressed the rewind button and rewound the whole roll of new film that had never even been used.

"Geez, Walda, we've got to take some pictures of this." Suddenly these pictures seemed to be an all-important life mission.

Taken aback by his reaction I said, "Tom, don't worry about it."

We sat in silence for the next couple of minutes. I looked at my watch. It was about 7:15. Then I saw someone I wanted to talk to and walked the few feet to say hello. When I came back, less than thirty seconds later, I saw something I will never, ever forget. That sight has burned itself into my memory and is something I think about every single day.

Tom sat, slumped forward in his chair. Thick foam gathered around his mouth and his pants were suddenly stained where he had just wet himself. His eyes rolled in the back of his head. His partial denture had come loose and his mouth hung open.

I was the first to see him, and then one by one, in less time than two heartbeats, everyone else noticed. For a moment, I stood paralyzed by fear. Someone's voice spurred me to move.

"Get him on his back!" someone yelled.

Somebody else shouted, "I'll call 911."

I ran to him and screamed. "Tom! Tom! Don't you dare leave me. We have so much to do. We have so much to do!"

Someone, I don't remember whom, came up behind me and placed their hands on my shoulders to comfort me. "Take it easy, Walda. Calm down. The EMTs will be here soon."

I shook my head mournfully. "My, God, he's gone. He's gone. He's had a heart attack. I know it's his heart."

Chapter 2

If Only I'd Known (Or Maybe I Did)

I thought about everything that had happened that day: his irritability; his behavior; his complaint of a pain in his chest. Suddenly, the puzzle pieces all fit together to form a morbid mosaic. That terrible game of "What if..." began to play in my mind. What if he had not exerted himself so much the day before? What if he had slept better the night before? What if he had not had so much to eat today? What if I had taken him to the hospital at the first sign of something wrong? What if? What if? What if? But I knew it was too late for "what ifs." Now I had to deal with what was.

People had helped Tom lie on the ground and I looked down at his seemingly lifeless form. Seeing Tom like that was too much for my mother and she left the scene in tears. Someone helped her onto my patio. She had always thought of Tom as the son she never had.

"It's not supposed to end like this," I sobbed. "It's not supposed to end like this for me, not for us." The tears flowed freely, and then I noticed his complexion changing color. With sad slowness, his face turned the deepest shade of purple I've ever seen.

Through the chaos, three wonderful friends, all nurses, Cindi, Jane, and Kirsten, knelt by his side to assess his condition.

"He's not breathing," Jane said and began administering CPR. Cindi and Kirsten immediately pitched in to help as did Ron Heggarty, another dear friend.

"Hey, Buddy, come back. Come on. Come on," Ron entreated with each compression to Tom's chest.

Jane captained the attempt to bring Tom back, her voice rising above the rest. "One and two and three and four and five. Breathe! One and two and three and four and five. Breathe!"

I waited, hands clasped to my breast in prayer, for something to happen, but after a minute or two, nothing did. Someone pounded on his chest. Someone else forced air into his lungs. Still, Tom would not breathe. Still, he had no pulse.

I stood by helplessly then fell to my knees as near to him as I could get. "Tom! Tom!" I shouted. "Please, come on! Fight! Come on, Tom! I need you! Come back, Tom! You can do it! Come on, Tom!"

As the ambulance siren, first distant, got closer, I could sense that Tom was going in and out of his body even during the resuscitation attempts. I alternated between feelings of apprehension, which in retrospect I knew was his, and serenity, which he later told me was his "astral" body holding me.

Suddenly, the EMTs appeared and dashed to where Tom still lay on the ground. "Back away, please," one EMT ordered as two others knelt beside Tom and began to work on him. Jane filled them in on what had happened and what she and her team had done for him.

"Tom!" I called and reached out to him. One EMT gently lifted me by the shoulders.

"I'm sorry, ma'am, but you're going to have to step back. We need room to work on him."

"But I'm his wife!" I protested.

"I understand, and I know you want to help. Right now he needs you to let us take care of him." He paused a moment to ascertain whether or not I understood what he had asked. "Okay?"

I nodded and let Kathy lead me a few feet away.

They administered CPR. They set up an IV drip. They injected drugs. All the while, they kept in radio contact with the hospital on their progress. Finally, forty minutes later one EMT looked up and said, "I've got a pulse."

My one and only thought was to thank God for this wonderful gift. He was still alive. My sister ran into the house to get my sneakers and purse while they transferred him into the ambulance. One of the EMTs asked, "Do you want to ride in the ambulance?"

I shook my head. "No, no. I'd probably just get in the way, and I can't bear to look at him with that color in his face."

I looked around at all the people standing by me and immediately knew Bob would be the right person to take me to the hospital. He and Kathy were very close to Tom and me and I knew Bob would be strong for me. I turned to Bob. My expression bore all the request I needed to utter.

"Anything I can do, Walda. Let's go." Bob reached for me. I needed his strength and I accepted his arm around my waist to hold me up. In turn, I wrapped my arm around him and he led the way down the street to his truck. With each step, I felt what little strength I had leave me, and my arm grew tighter around my friend. I was so grateful for him because I knew that without him, I couldn't have made it. By the time we reached his truck, my legs felt as if they were leaden weights. The only thing holding me up was Bob's strength. Then the grief hit me.

The only way I can describe that awful feeling is to say that somewhere deep in the pit of my stomach, a coldness, an emptiness appeared. With deliberate slowness and efficacy, it spread to my legs and arms and head. By the time we reached Bob's truck, its icy tentacles had extended to my heart and mind, tightening every muscle in my body as though I were readying myself for battle.

Overwhelmed by the feeling, my heart rate accelerated and my breathing grew shallow. Bob must have noticed the sudden change in me.

"Are you all right?" he asked as he opened the passenger door for me.

I climbed up into the seat and looked across at my friend. "Bob, he's not going make it. I just know he's not going to make it." I said, "I should think positive thoughts but I can't honestly see him coming through this." Wordlessly, Bob closed the door and walked around to the other side.

The five-minute drive to Lawrence General Hospital seemed like five hours, the longest five minutes of my life. Heart pounding and head spinning, I didn't see the people I knew filled the streets. I didn't hear the traffic noise. My mind focused on the ambulance just minutes ahead of me rushing Tom to the hospital. Neither of us ever expected this. He was always so healthy, so alive, and so young. Too young for this to be happening.

Chapter 3

My Father's Final Gift

I was born in 1952 and grew up in a small town in eastern Massachusetts, in a loving yet somewhat dysfunctional family. At the age of fourteen, I met Tom. Even at that tender age, I knew he was my soul mate. Our love grew and before I knew it, we were married in a beautiful church ceremony in 1972. I became pregnant with our son right away and Tom worked two, sometimes three jobs to support us. Despite being so young, we remained focused on our goals, and eventually saved enough to buy a home.

Throughout the years, I enjoyed my role as wife and mother and thought I had everything I wanted. Although many people told us our marriage would never work, we settled into a comfortable rut, but something seemed to be missing. And although we were good, moral people, we really never gave much of a thought to anyone but ourselves. What mattered to us was the financial stability to fulfill our goals. When our son, Tommy, reached middle school age, I decided that my part-time waitress job had taken its toll and that a better career waited, so I enrolled in a Business Management course at a local college.

In 1985, I got my real estate license, and in 1989, was offered a plum job with a high-tech communications company in Burlington—great money and a chance to prove what I could do in the business world. They say that life is what happens while you're busy making other plans, and in 1992 life happened! My husband and I were both laid off from our high-paying jobs and thrust into the unemployment lines. Bang— just like that! No warning, no time to plan.

Traumatized by the enormity of the situation, I sank into a deep depression. I walked around in a fog, hating everything and blaming everyone I could think of, including God, for this cruel unfairness. But some niggling little voice inside me kept saying, "Come on, girl, this isn't the way to go!" My spirit was screaming. Unfortunately, human nature is such that we don't seek answers or guidance when things are running smoothly. It's only when everything falls apart—or seems to— that we look to a higher source for the reasons why.

My spiritual journey had begun.

Things started falling into my lap—books, movies, videos, TV shows on every subject from angels to synchronicity. Topics that I would have scoffed at just a few weeks earlier now fascinated me. I met a woman named Helen Rose, a gifted spiritual teacher, who reminded me of the joys in life and ignited the flame of my soul's quest for answers. I began meditating and three weeks later, began to see a difference. My husband noticed that I was whistling and singing again—not just happy but joyful! I no longer "sweated the small stuff," and began a mission to forgive anyone who had hurt me in the past. I learned to love myself and forgive myself for my past mistakes by recognizing that I'd done the best I could at the time. I was no longer angry or depressed. I was more focused on the situations at hand. I was dealing with what had been given to me instead of constantly whining, why me? I was calmer and stress was no longer the six-letter word that ruled my life. And because I was willing to let go of the past and listen to my inner voice, many wonderful things started to happen.

In 1993, I landed a high level position as Director of Sales for IDG World Expo in Framingham, Massachusetts. In 1995, I launched my own consulting firm, which offered sales planning and development services to a variety of businesses. Even though things were looking up, I continued my search for answers with a passion. I was amazed at the changes in my outlook on life. I went from being selfish, angry and confused to being loving, compassionate and non-judgmental.

In August of 1995, my father passed away after almost a year of debilitating illness. Holding him in my arms as he died, I watched his spirit slip out of his body on its journey into the next world. My father and I had never been close, and had had our share of disagreements over the years. But as a grandfather, he mellowed out and both my son and my nephew were blessed by his love and wisdom. My sister and I stayed with him round the clock in his last few months, during which he taught me the meaning of unconditional love and forgiveness. I forgave him for all the hurt and let it go.

Seeing his spirit at the moment of death sparked my curiosity about death and dying, and prompted the thought about possibly working with the dying as my life's mission. There's nothing to all this death stuff, I thought. I was able to detach myself from being emotional, so I could feed him, hold his hand, and whisper words of encouragement. I was an expert. There was nothing more to learn. Or so I thought.

Chapter 4

Reprieve and Game Over

Once at the hospital, we ran into the emergency room and told the nurse who we were. "Oh, yes, they're on their way in now. Why don't you wait in here," she suggested, ushering us into a small waiting room off the emergency room. I shuddered. The plain, white walls and stark, institutional furniture told me I was in a very sad, cold place. A small television set, volume down, perched on a high corner shelf. A few religious pictures hung on the walls. Boxes of tissues carelessly tossed on the small tables only added to the macabre atmosphere, sad reminders of all the grief-stricken families that had passed through this room and felt as I did.

Thankfully, before I even had a chance to sit down, one of the nurses from the emergency room came in and said, "They've brought your husband in."

"How's he doing?"

"Not well, I'm afraid. He's not responding and he has a very weak pulse. We're starting him on some medications but he's arresting every five minutes and we're coding him. He's not coming back well and he's slipped into a very deep coma. They've called in a neurologist to examine him but it doesn't look good. From what they can see right now, he has severe heart damage. We need to stabilize him before we can do any more. I don't recommend you coming in just yet."

"Is his color any better?" I asked wringing my hands.

Her voice softened. "Yes, it's better."

I had nothing more to ask. I had more nothing to say. Nothing more to do. I turned to Bob and cried on his shoulder. I held his hand and he wrapped his other arm around me. I nestled into the comfort and warmth he offered. His being there meant so much to me. When I finally gained some semblance of control, I looked up into his face to see he was fighting back tears of his own.

"Bob, I forgot to tell him I loved him this morning," I sobbed. "It can't happen this way. It's not supposed to happen this way."

"He knows you love him, Walda, even if you didn't say it this morning. He knows. Trust me."

I decided it was time to call Tom's family. The clock on the wall said 8:30. An hour-and-a-half had already passed since this nightmare began. I knew that my sister-in-law Marsha would begin the family telephone tree and within minutes, everyone would have the news.

"Hello," Marsha's voice brought me out of my thought.

"Marsha, this is Walda." My voiced wavered.

"What's the matter? What's wrong?"

"I'm at Lawrence General Hospital. Tom's had a massive heart attack and it doesn't look good. They don't think he's going to make it. The family needs to come now. Could you please call everyone?"

"Right away. I'll be there as soon as I can," she said and hung up the phone.

"I have to get out of this room," I said and walked into the hall. I found a nurse who directed me to the chapel upstairs and there I gave Tom the only help I could. Alone, in the dim light of the tiny chapel, I sank to my knees and prayed. When the words came from my heart, I remembered an old saying I'd heard time and time again: "Be careful what you pray for because you just might get it." For that reason, my prayers did not include the plea to let Tom live.

I prayed to God, the Divine Source, for the highest and best for everyone involved and for the wisdom to bring us all closer to His Light. I was so afraid to pray for Tom to live because for as long as he'd not been breathing, I had a feeling that if he did pull through, he'd be so mentally impaired that he'd have wished for death. Yes, he'd still be breathing, but that might be all. I couldn't be that selfish.

I prayed for Tom's safety, his comfort, and his peace. I asked the light of God to care for him, ease his pain, and to carry him home. Then I prayed for the strength to deal with what was happening to me. I needed to stay in control and keep my family together.

Casual acquaintances can't believe that I, a skeptic in so many ways, could have given Tom and myself over to the Divine Source so completely. What they don't know is the strength to do that didn't come overnight, nor did it arrive at the hospital with the ambulance. It had been a long process of spiritual exploration, a spiritual journey.

I returned to the waiting room and a few minutes later, Marsha and her husband Junior arrived. I opened my arms to her and we hugged as we've never hugged before.

As the predictable questions tumbled out of Marsha, "When did this happen? How did this happen? Had Tom been sick? Had he been to the doctor? How bad was it?" I fought back the tears and answered the best I could. While I had faith, that did not ease the pain in my heart. And when I'd told her all I could, we cried together.

During the next hour, other family members arrived, a blur of faces filling the room, crying, hugging and kissing. We held hands, cried together and comforted each other, opening our arms and our hearts to each other, offering what solace and warmth we could. A husband, a brother, a friend lay in a room just down the hall, and we all hoped and prayed for the best.

One of the security guards brought in a tray of coffee for us and I knew then that things were bad. "You may need this. You may be here a while," he warned. I took a cup from the tray and settled in to wait. About a half hour later, a nurse and a doctor came into the waiting room.

"Mrs. Woods?" the doctor said, leafing through the charts on his clipboard.

"How is he?" I asked rising from my chair. The sudden silence in the room pressed in around me, punctuated only by the ticking of the wall-clock.

"Mrs. Woods, he's very sick. He's sustained substantial damage to his heart. Right now, he's in a coma."

"How did this happen? Why didn't we have any warning? He was so incredibly healthy. How could this happen?"

He shook his head. "I honestly don't know. My best guess is that Tom was experiencing small pains from time to time but he ignored the warning signs. Then when it hit, it hit with a vengeance."

In a barely audible whisper, I asked the question that had to be asked, "Will he live?"

"Right now, it will be a miracle if he makes it through the night. I've sent for a neurologist to evaluate him because, in cases like this, patients often suffer brain damage as well because the brain has been deprived of oxygen.

"When you saw Tom having his heart attack, most likely he was already dead. When someone has a massive heart attack, they're generally killed instantly. The effects of the attack, what you saw, the aspirating, the spasms, was his body actually shutting down. Those are things that happen that we don't have any control over.

"The emergency room staff has stabilized him and done all they can for him. They're getting ready to take him up to the Cardiac Care Unit, where we can do more."

The doctor's prognosis only confirmed what I already knew in my heart. Tom was not going to make it.

What happened after that is a blur of crying and trying to bring myself under control—until the next bout of tears. In between, I tried to comfort the family while fighting hard to put my own feelings on hold. At one point, I told myself it was important not to feel anything, to become numb, because that was the only way I was going to get through this tragedy.

My sister-in-law Karen came over to me and put her arm around my shoulder. "Come on, let's go out and have a smoke."

I nodded and as we walked toward the door, a nurse called out, "Mrs. Woods, they're taking your husband up now."

I shook my head at the implied invitation. I didn't want to see him, not yet. I couldn't bear the pain. Why play the hero and throw my body over his, telling him I loved him. If he couldn't hear me, it didn't matter whether I did it or not. And if he could hear me, it might terrify him.

I went outside and had a smoke with my sister-in-law. I figured they needed a few minutes to get him settled in. The cool evening air and a cigarette helped me compose myself to lead the family upstairs.

The nurse on duty nodded and smiled as we entered the CCU.

"Can I see him now?" I asked.

"One visitor at a time and only family," the nurse whispered as she pointed to the door through which they had taken Tom.

I placed my hand over the doorknob and with my face only inches from the glass, I took a deep breath and steeled myself for the sight I both dreaded and loved at the same time. I wanted to see Tom, the man I loved, the man I called friend, my life's partner. A man full of life and love and laughter. But I dreaded seeing him now, lying in a bed at death's door.

I took a deep breath and briskly opened the door. I gasped at what I saw. Doctors and nurses worked furiously, attaching IV lines, electrodes, wires, tubes, and adjusting machines. I couldn't believe the mountain of equipment they had hooked into him. The machines took up so much space, I couldn't get anywhere near his face.

In the nearly thirty years we'd been together, the man who took my breath away had never had more than a cold, and now he lay, eyes closed, kept alive by machines, his chest rising and falling to the beat of the respirator. He didn't strike me as being at peace. I knew that while he might not be aware of what was going on around him, I sensed his fear. Did he know what had happened to him or where he was, I wondered. Tom, who had always comforted me and allayed my fears, now needed me and my help, and I had none to give.

Suddenly the room closed in on me, and I had to leave. Back in the waiting room, I sat staring straight ahead, trying to come to terms with what had happened. One by one, family members took turns visiting Tom, and each in turn, returned to the waiting room, ashen-faced, shaken and stunned at what they'd seen.

Marsha sat beside me. "Have you called Tommy yet?"

I shook my head.

"You want me to call him for you?" she offered.

"No, I'm not going to call him now."

"Walda, you have to call him," she insisted. "Tom's his father."

"Look, it's after one in the morning. What good would it do to call him now? He'd only worry. I'll call him in the morning."

She nodded and settled back into the chair in silence. Soon, almost everyone had left and I remained in the waiting room with Marsha.

The clock on the wall ticked the hours by. At 1:30, another doctor came in and offered his hand. "Mrs. Woods, I'm Doctor Basu, the neurologist. Doctor Curtis sent for me. I've just run some tests on your husband." He paused a moment as though looking for just the right words.

"And?" I asked, encouraging him to say something else. The optimist in me battled the realist.

"He's not brain dead," he began.

I breathed an audible sigh of relief until he continued.

"However, he has quite a bit of brain damage and has slipped into a very deep coma. I think they've coded him thirty times since they brought him in. I've conferred with the cardiologist, Doctor Curtis, and he agrees with me that if Tom does come out of this, and there's only a very slight chance of that, that he will be permanently mentally impaired."

I was afraid to ask the next obvious question. "How mentally impaired?"

"He may not know his name or who you are. He may require twenty-four hour care to do the simplest things like eating and going to the bathroom."

A sob escaped from me as I sank back. Dr. Basu sat beside me.

"I'm sorry, Mrs. Woods. I wish I had better news for you."

"So do I, but I know Tom wouldn't want to live like that. How long does he have?" I asked.

"There's no telling. I think he could go at anytime," the doctor said softly.

With a crumpled tissue, I wiped away new tears. Suddenly, memories of the recent loss of my father flooded me. He had been so ill for so long that finally we had signed a "Do Not Resuscitate" order for him. As painful as it might be for me, I knew what I had to do now. "I'd like to you to put a DNR on him."

The doctor nodded. "I understand. I'll write it on his chart and inform the staff. We won't resuscitate him again if he slips away." He rose and offered me his hand. "I'm really very sorry."

"Well, that's it," I said, resigning myself to the situation. "He's trying to tell us to let him go."

I looked around at the bland white walls that surrounded me and suddenly felt sick to my stomach. "I've got to go home. I can't stay here by myself and I can't ask anyone to stay with me. Please call me if something happens, Doctor, and I'll be back in a few hours."

I went in to see Tom once more and an army of doctors and nurses still surrounded him so I couldn't get very close to him. Instead, I touched his leg, sent his soul a kiss, and left.

When I arrived home, my mother and Jason were sound asleep. One reason I wanted to come home was to check on my mother. Satisfied, I went downstairs to the family room and watched TV. At the moment, the idea of sleep sounded wonderful, but an unobtainable luxury. My mind raced, replaying all the unheeded warning signs during the day, hoping a new dawn would wake me from this nightmare, but I knew this was no horror engineered by my imagination. This was reality.

Instead of trying to sleep, I channel-surfed and landed on an "I Love Lucy" rerun. The old black and white pictures cast a strange flickering light on the darkened walls, but they were just patterns. My mind was elsewhere. All I could think about was Tom and what had happened to him, what had happened to us. Then I suddenly realized, I'm grieving.

The next morning, a miracle happened. Against all odds, Tom had come out of his coma. I rushed to the hospital and found Pauline, the nurse who had called me. "How is he?"

"He's responding but he's still very sick. He's on a respirator so he won't be able to talk to you, but he can mouth words and nod his head. He even squeezed my hand and blinked."

Grateful for this small favor, I broke down in tears. Pauline handed me a box of tissues and I dabbed at my eyes.

"Let me get it together. I can't go in there like this." I didn't want him to worry about me. Once in control again, I went in. I could see he was excited to see me. He moved his head back and forth, and opened his eyes wide.

I drew as near to him as I could. "Hi, Babe. How you doin'?"

He blinked.

"Tom, do you remember what happened?"

He shook his head.

I said, "You had a heart attack at the cook-out. You're very sick, but you can come home in a few weeks if you take care of yourself and do what the doctors and nurses tell you. You have to take care of yourself." His eyes filled with sadness and I felt almost resignation coming from him. At that point, I was sure he wasn't going to make it, and that the only reason he'd come back was to say good-bye to me. His spirit may have even felt me grieving, even heard me say that I hadn't told him I loved him that morning. How grateful I was for this one last time together to say good-bye.

Him coming out of the coma was too good to be true, and I didn't allow myself to buy into the optimism. While I would have loved for him to recover, I was also a realist, and decided to expect the best, but be prepared for the worst. I was here to say good-bye.

I reached for the hand of the man who was my every breath, my hero, my knight in shining armor, a part of me, and my very best friend in the world. His flesh was clammy and cold, reminding me of death. I wanted to touch him, but felt uncomfortable doing it, so I placed the sheet between our hands. "There, that will keep you warmer," I demurred.

Suddenly his color improved, his eyes were alert and responding. "Squeeze my hand, honey," I whispered.

He did and I smiled at him, fighting back the tears that threatened to burst out. "That's great. I love you."

He mouthed the same words. He was still here, but he seemed edgy. He couldn't seem to keep still.

"What's the matter?"

His lips formed the word "thirsty."

The nurse who had been in the room said, "He's very thirsty, but we can't give him anything by mouth. But you can swab his mouth out with these little sponges."

She handed me a three-inch-long stick with a small sponge the size of a cotton ball at the end. She brought me a cup of ice chips and some water and I doused the swab in the water and put it in his mouth. He was so desperately thirsty that he sucked on that little sponge as if his life depended on it. In the next thirty minutes, I must have used twenty of those swabs. Then he mouthed the word, "hot."

Outside in the waiting room, I found a copy of *Time* magazine to fan him with. As the cooling air blew past his body, I saw the gratitude in his face. I smiled encouragement, trying not to stare at the little hole in his chest where the doctors had intubated him the night before. I tried desperately to shut out the pain that threatened to engulf me.

He tried to get up but was too weak. He kept moving his arms and legs, trying to hoist himself up.

The nurse came in. "Mr. Woods, you've got to rest. I'm going to give you something to help you sleep."

Crisply, she gave him the injection and slowly, he closed his eyes. Silently, I said my good-byes and left.

Despite the fact that Tom had awoken from the coma, within the next few hours he slipped back into the depths of unconsciousness. It was now only a matter of time. For the next two days, Tom's family and I cried together. Tommy came home from school and we exchanged all the love and comfort we could muster. We kept silent vigil and grieved and prayed. We paced the CCU waiting room and sank exhausted onto the cold vinyl couches to catch a few fitful minutes of sleep, only to wake again and repeat the seemingly endless cycle.

We took turns with him, hoping he knew we were there and that he heard what we said. Every time I thought of my strong, brave Tom lying so pathetically still in that bed, tears welled in my eyes, pain coming from somewhere deep inside me, a place I never knew existed. It filled my whole being. I was in mourning, but tried to shake the feeling. After all, Tom hadn't died—not yet. He was still among the living and I told myself that where there was life, there was hope. But the tears still came. I never lost total control or became hysterical, but I cried because this sudden cruel blow had come out of the blue. We'd made a game of planning for our future together, and this had never been a part of it. I thought of all the dreams we'd shared and all the things we'd started together that would never be finished. My grief turned to anger and resentment at his being snatched from me while I could do nothing but watch helplessly. IT JUST WASN'T SUPPOSED TO BE LIKE THIS FOR US!

On one occasion, as he lay in a coma and I sat at his bedside, I "heard" him say, "I am not in that body anymore. I am on my way with the angels to another place, but I will stay with you as long as I can. I do not wish for you to see me die. Please remember me as healthy, not the shell that lies in that bed."

Describing how this communication felt is difficult. It was an inner "knowing," as if he had somehow blended with me. My body vibrated gently from the inside out, and I could hear a faint "buzzing." When I closed my eyes, it was as if I was watching a movie screen on which I saw Tom embracing me. I could "see" his spirit going back and forth, in and out of his body. His words and thoughts were not audible but were more like an interruption to my own thoughts. I could hear them in my head the same way I hear myself when I'm thinking. I know I was not making those thoughts up, since I didn't want to hear what he was telling me. But as real as it seemed, it took me some time to accept what was happening.

At other times, the memories would flood in on me. All our happy times. How his face lit up when he saw me. His goofy grin. The way he touched me that sent a shiver down the length of my body.

The clock said 4:15 p.m. when a gut-wrenching wail pulled me from my reverie. It was as if someone had been torn in half. Tom's brother, Dan, was in with him, and Tommy and I looked at each other. We knew immediately. Tom was gone.

Chapter 5

Help Arrives

I returned home, the grieving widow, but Tom had other ideas. First, two of the clocks had stopped at 4:15, the time of his death. Then I smelled his after-shave and the "feel" of his presence. My electric clock/radio began to turn on and off by itself. The phone often rang once and when I answered it, all I heard was white noise, like the static between radio stations. Light bulbs burned out faster than they should, and no sooner did I change them, they'd burn out again.

In the days following Tom's death, I was thankful for the past few years of spiritual preparation. As I explained earlier, my awakening began in December of 1991. Tom had come home from work one day with the unthinkable news—ninety-days notice! A corporate takeover had forced his employer of fifteen-years to bring in non-union workers. Tom was devastated because, as with most men, his job was a major part of his self-definition, and this blow annihilated his self-esteem.

Trying to make him feel better, I chirped, "Look at it this way, you've been wanting to take a little time off. Now's your chance. I'm still working. We'll be fine."

One month later, in 1992, I was laid off from my job. Talk about a double-whammy! We had a little money set aside for a rainy day, but this was a hurricane. We commiserated over each other's losses and after a month of worry, I began to think that there had to be some bizarre reason for this, and I felt compelled to find it. Although I tried to remain calm and cope with things rationally, sometimes the situation overwhelmed me.

Sleep eluded me and I watched a lot of late-night TV. Fascinated by an infomercial touting a "psychic hotline," I started calling because I thought they might have some answers for me. But all I got was a $300 phone bill. What a waste of money, I thought, especially now. I wasn't going to find what I needed that way. Somehow synchronicity sends us what we need when we need it the most, and that's when I met Helen Rose.

A friend recommended that I speak with her, and when I did, I suddenly felt a strong connection to this woman who called herself a spiritual counselor. She charged me almost nothing for a reading and I began calling her weekly. I was still searching, still struggling, and my spirit was screaming for something, but I had no idea for what. To my dismay, Helen Rose didn't have all the answers either, but she did put me on the right track to finding them for myself.

She did four very important things for me: she reminded me of the spiritual side of life; she introduced me to meditation; she ignited my interest in angels, and she recommended some books she thought I might learn from.

I took her advice, and the information opened up a whole new world to me. Before the upheaval, I'd never even thought about such subjects as angels or meditation, much less considered them worthy of serious consideration. As far as I was concerned, they weren't even topics of casual conversation. I always just said, "That's not for me! I don't want to hear it," and stopped the conversation right there.

I suppose my ego just wasn't ready for it. But now, when I needed answers and a new perspective on the slew of problems life cast in our direction, I tried it out of sheer desperation. If others had no answers for me, perhaps I could find them somewhere within.

I became totally fascinated by angels and who they were, where they came from, why they were created, and what they do and don't do. I learned that each of us has been given at least one guardian angel (or spirit guide) to guide us through life, to comfort us spiritually when we need it, to guide us, and to rejoice with us and for us, as we grow closer to the Divine Source. Everyone has them, regardless of religious belief.

As guardians, they protect us from spiritual and in many cases, physical danger. They comfort us in times of need by reminding us of Universal Love. They don't predict the future and they can't change our direction. Our free will makes us totally responsible for the actions we choose, but they can and do give us signs to nudge us in the direction that's best for us at the time.

I learned that at least one guardian angel follows us throughout our life, but additional angels come in at certain times. At any one time, we may have as many as fifteen or twenty guiding and protecting us. They come to us at different points in our lives for different reasons, and when their work is done, they step back, but never leave us completely. They're always there should we need them, and if we are ever able to communicate with them, we are truly blessed.

One night, I'd been meditating and was drifting into sleep when I became acutely aware of another presence in my thoughts. Someone was there with me, in my mind. Then he spoke. "My name is Noel. I've been with you for many years. In fact, I've been with you through many different lifetimes, including one during the French Revolution, in which you were the daughter of a ship-builder."

Initially, I was awestruck. Why would such a mystical experience happen to me? But then I began to focus on his words, wanting to "hear" everything he had to say. For ten minutes, Noel placed thoughts in my mind, teaching me, soothing my thirsty spirit. Before he left, he said, "Trust in me. I will be here. Know that my presence is always with you and that I'll be sending you signs. Keep your mind open so that I may shine through."

I flashed back to something that happened to me when I was maybe 17 that has always puzzled me. I was dating Tom and we'd fallen asleep in front of the TV at his apartment. I woke up, looked at my watch, and cried, "Oh, my gosh, it's nearly three!"

"Walda, it's too late to drive home. Why don't you just spend the night?"

I shook my head. "Good Lord, no! I can't do that!"

I grabbed my things and ran for the car. I was too tired to be driving, but had to get home before my father returned at four. I must have fallen asleep at the wheel because I woke up with a start, my foot hard down on the brake. I dreamed that a man was walking across the road and I slammed on the brakes to avoid hitting him.

Shaken and breathless, I looked up and down the narrow, twisty mountain road, but saw no one. Little of the road had a guardrail, so I could easily have plunged off the road into a deep ravine, so I reasoned that I'd had some type of spiritual assistance. I asked Noel about that incident, and he confirmed that he was responsible for the dream because it was not yet time for me to leave this world. So he woke me and kept me safe.

Since that first night, Noel has stayed with me, teaching me, guiding me. I couldn't wait for our nightly sessions. I discovered that I could request his presence during meditation. At one point, he allowed me to see him in my mind.

Most memorable were his clear blue eyes, like ice but without the chill. I found warmth and strength in those eyes, and at the same time they were magnificent and mesmerizing. I felt unworthy to even look into them. His face, framed by very light hair, was extremely handsome, and his clothes floated about him like a cloud. We embraced and talked, but from time to time, I had to look away because his magnificence overwhelmed me.

Noel urged me to find the Divine Light within myself and to reach out to people more often. I began a more compassionate lifestyle, more tolerant than I ever thought possible. Slowly, my anger and resentment dissipated. I felt great!

Then he taught me to meditate in a different way. At one session he said to me, "You're not relaxing enough."

I said, "I rest every day. I always try to rest."

"There's a difference between resting and relaxing. Resting is watching television, reading, and anything else that is not *work*. True relaxation comes from the soul, from shifting your consciousness to a different level of awareness. Your physical body becomes non-existent to the mind and there are no encumbrances to detain you from exploring the oneness of the Universe.

Suddenly, I understood, and that became a point of focus for me. I wasn't allowing myself to relax as strongly as I should in my meditations and I began to change my technique. Even now when I meditate, I thank Noel for showing me how to alter my consciousness and go deep inside of my soul.

He also suggested I surround myself with white light, and say a prayer for protection before meditating, something I'd never done before. "A prayer for protection is always necessary when you alter your consciousness so that nothing comes between you and the Divine Source," he said.

Chapter 6

More Answers

I began an intense study of prayer and meditation, and how they work together. I practiced relaxation techniques, and learned how to go deep into a part of myself that I had never explored before. Some call it the soul, others the subconscious mind. Whatever you call it, it exists, it's real, and it has answers.

My interest in the metaphysical also sparked a renewed interest in spirituality. Never a religious person, I'd always had a deep faith that some type of Supreme Being existed and desired to know this Universal Intelligence. I've never been an active member of any church because the thought of gathering with others to worship a common God held no attraction for me. Keeping Him in my heart was enough. But I wanted to know *my* God. I knew by now that love and fear could not exist together so who or what was this Entity I had grown to love *and* fear? And how could my past interpretation have become so tangled with contradictions?

No one religion, book, or philosophy ever gave me all the answers. Somehow, they all lacked some vital information to answer the questions that plagued me, particularly after Tom died, such as, "How can I make sense of what's happened?" "Why *do* bad things happen to good people?" "Why am I here?"

What I didn't realize at the time is that these questions had no concrete answers. I was looking to make sense of the world, a world where Nature follows the laws set forth by its Creator, yet where random acts of violence and death occur despite the "rules." Since I could not find the answers outside myself, I searched within through prayer and meditation.

Two small sentences changed how I think: "Prayer is talking to God. Meditation is listening." Suddenly the lights in my mind went on. I saw the "give-and-take" with the Divine, and how the two techniques can be used together.

From my belief that angels were guiding me, and from the peace I found in meditation, I was able to begin detaching from the fear I'd felt

for most of my life. It was soon replaced with complete and unconditional love for the Universal Intelligence and the new relationship I was
building with its oneness. I found that the more I practiced this new
spirituality, the more mystical my experiences became.

Something happened during this phase of rediscovery that I will
never forget. I'd become concerned that I tended to judge others too
quickly with first impressions. If I didn't like people at our first meeting,
it didn't matter what they did after that, I was stuck with my dislike for
them. I expressed this concern to Noel and resolved not to judge people
so hastily.

A couple of days later when I awoke, I looked over at Tom and
noticed a glow around him, much like a rainbow. Of course, I just stared,
open-mouthed.

"What? What are you staring at?" he asked when he saw the stunned
expression on my face.

"You!"

"You're looking at me as if you've never seen me before," he said.

"You know, you have colors all around you. In fact, you have two
different colors just there," I exclaimed, pointing to his head. "Go look
in the mirror and see if you can see them."

From the bathroom, I heard his voice, "I don't know what you were
dreaming about, Walda, but I don't see anything."

He stood in the bathroom doorway, and asked, "So are the colors
still there?"

Just as I said, "Yes," the glow began to fade and, after a few minutes,
had completely gone.

I had no idea what the colors were all about. I questioned my eye-
sight and briefly my grip on reality. But it occurred to me that this had
been perhaps another metaphysical occurrence. I figured one mystical
experience was probably enough for a lifetime, so I pushed it to the back
of my mind. I wasn't even thinking about the light around Tom when I
left for work that morning, but when I saw a neighbor heading for her
car, she, too, was surrounded by glowing colors. Again, I just stared.

"Walda, are you all right?" she asked as we talked.

I know I wore my wonder on my face and quickly changed my expression. "Er ... I just wanted to say I love that outfit you've got on today."

She looked down at her suit then back at me. "You've seen it a hundred times, Walda. What's going on?"

How could I tell her a rainbow of colors surrounded her? "Nothing. I guess I'm just tired." And as we said our good-byes, the colors faded.

For the rest of the day, everyone had colors, different of course, but they moved with the person and lasted only a few minutes before fading from view. By the end of the day, I'd learned not to stare, but still had no idea what was happening to me.

That night, I asked Noel, "What exactly happened to me today? What was I seeing?"

"You were seeing auras."

I had read about auras, so the next logical question was, "I never saw them before. Why now?"

"You wanted a way to judge people more fairly when you met them, so I helped you develop the ability to see their aura. The aura is the energy of the spirit. You can tell much about a person from the colors in their aura." Then he explained that a person's aura changes color constantly, depending on their emotional and physical health at any given moment.

"I've helped you develop the tool. Now it's up to you to learn how to use it." A few years later, I finally found a book that explained the fifty or sixty different colors that can make up an aura. At first, I thought it was a neat gift, but after a while, it proved too distracting, so I learned to block the ability, summoning it only when needed.

At Noel's urging, I intensified my study of the metaphysical and paranormal and began using what I learned to help others. Some people might call it "New Age" philosophy, a term that's hardly accurate since most of what people call "New Age" has been with us for thousands of years! We'll return to this topic in Part Two.

Chapter 7

The Antics Begin

W hen Tom died, I wondered if he was all right. Then I wondered about where he was and what he was doing. The next logical step followed. If Tom really were alive, just in another dimension, would it be possible to communicate with him? One question led to another, and I hungered for the knowledge.

Tom and I have always shared a deep loving bond and I knew with certainty that his death hadn't changed this. So could we break through the barrier that separated us and continue our connection?

Researchers tell us that we only use about ten percent of our brain's capacity, and that every one of us has the ability to perceive things outside the five physical senses—a sixth sense, if you will. Most of us go through life totally ignorant of the dormant power we possess and make no attempt to tap into it. A few people are born with this capacity already turned on, but anyone can develop the talent, and refine and perfect it.

Some claim they can communicate with spirits in other dimensions or that they actually visit them there. Admittedly, most are frauds and have no more power to communicate with spirits than my kitchen chair. But a few can genuinely reach out to grieving survivors and make the connection with those on the so-called "other side." Even those who do not believe in spirit communication, yet accept the concept of an afterlife, must concede that there is overwhelming evidence that those who have passed on still exist.

I had always been skeptical of such things, dismissing them as so much nonsense and imagination, but after Tom died, my feelings on the subject changed, especially when I felt him so close to me and received signs of his presence. At first, whenever something unusual happened, I'd look for some rational explanation. It wasn't that I didn't want to believe, but the skeptic in me said, "Look, if this is really a sign from Tom, it's got to be much more magnificent." But as the occurrences continued on a regular basis, rational explanations for them became harder. And they did become more magnificent.

Things began to happen the day after Tom died, even before his funeral. It started with the phone. It would ring once and when I picked it up, all I heard was a static hiss, much like the sound of an off-station radio. Although it happened frequently, I reasoned that something was wrong with the phone.

Light bulbs flickered, but even though I replaced them, they continued to flicker. The TV turned on and off by itself and changed stations. But the incident that finally convinced me these were signs from Tom happened while my nephew, Jason, and I were watching a movie on the *Lifetime Channel.* I've always enjoyed the programs on *Lifetime* and Tom would tease me with, "Oh, Walda, you always love to watch those sissy things."

Jason and I were deeply involved in a movie when suddenly the TV switched to a football game, one of Tom's passions. Then, the volume increased. The cable company could find nothing wrong, so suspecting that a neighbor's remote was interfering with mine, I went through three different remote controls. Still, the channels switched of their own accord. Figuring the fault lay with the television set, I bought a new one, but the phenomenon continued. This had to be more than an electrical problem. In the end, I gave up, and each time a football game or a basketball game suddenly replaced the program I'd been watching, I just smiled and said, "Tom, I know you're here and I still love you." Then I switched back to my program and continued to watch without incident.

A curious event occurred when I went to Texas to visit a friend. Only six weeks had passed since Tom died and the October weather was just beautiful. The air was cool and crisp, and I had all the windows open. Tom had always preferred keeping everything closed.

Before I left for the airport, I closed all the windows, except for the upstairs, which I left open just an inch to keep the air circulating. Kathy, my neighbor, would bring in my mail, feed the cats, and watch the house while I was gone.

I returned four days later to find the house hot and stifling. Then I noticed that the upstairs windows were closed. I immediately called Kathy and asked, "Please tell me you closed my upstairs windows."

"I didn't touch them. Why? Should I have closed them?" she asked.

Neither of us had any logical explanation, so I knew this was Tom's way of getting my attention, a reminder of the life we'd shared for so many years.

Not long afterward, I was downstairs in the family room looking at a beautiful album of photos of Tom that Kathy had put together for me. When I went upstairs, every light on the second floor was blazing—the stove light, the kitchen light, the bathroom, the dining room, both living room lights, even the outside lights. Every light on the third floor was on, too, including a light in my son's room that had never worked, and a light on the underside of my new dresser's mirror that I never knew even existed!

Suddenly, the odd waves of emotion shifted to the most incredible feelings of love and peace, further proof that Tom was close by. I told him how blessed I was to have him come to me like this. My legs turned to jelly. I know that if I could have seen my house from the outside, it would have been pulsating with light. As I went from room to room, shutting off all the lights, I couldn't help but be amazed at the ways Tom found to reassure me of his presence and his love.

Tom's favorite means of communication, however, was the television. It would turn off and on without anyone being near either it or the remote control. Curiously, it would turn off and on exactly on the hour, according to the cable box digital clock. As I mentioned earlier, it would also change channels on its own. I would be watching a favorite program and suddenly a sporting event (Tom's favorite) would replace it. I swapped cable remotes three times, and even bought a brand new TV set, but not only did the occurrences continue, they became even more frequent!

Friends and family experienced many of these events with me, and even the most hardcore skeptics attest to them. One night, a group of us was playing cards when the chandelier, on a dimmer switch, suddenly came on fully. But then it became even brighter! And brighter still, until finally the bulbs exploded! No one had moved from the table to touch the switch.

Tom signals his presence to me in a number of other ways. Sometimes, I sense his presence so intensely that it literally takes my breath away! And I finally figured out that when I felt my body "vibrating," he was embracing me. Many times, he chooses to speak to me through music, and I'll suddenly feel an overwhelming urge to turn on the radio, only to hear a song whose words convey how Tom is feeling.

In the beginning, when all this started, I was worried that I was on the brink of a breakdown. I wanted it to be true, but could it really be Tom, or was I deluding myself? What was I supposed to make of all this?

As amazing and comforting as Tom's tricks were, I was at a loss as to what to do. Some of my friends told me that there's never been any credible evidence of an afterlife, yet after all the books and research, I just couldn't agree. Undisputable facts and credible testimony from millions of people gradually eroded my skepticism, and I decided that, until it could be proven that there *wasn't* life after death, I would remain undaunted in my search for answers.

Then I saw her ... and my life would never be the same. It happened one day as I was surfing the TV channels and happened on a rerun of a national talk show first aired in 1994. Titled "Spirit Communications," the featured guest that day was psychic medium Patricia Mischell. Of course, I was transfixed.

Patricia brought messages to the studio audience from loved ones. Her sincere ability to reach out to people and comfort them impressed me so that even before the show was over, I called her office. I was told that Patricia was booked up for four months, but that due to a cancellation, I could have a telephone appointment the next day! I was ecstatic! Maybe now I would be given the guidance I so desperately needed. All I had to do was send, by overnight mail, my husband's name and date of death, along with a photo of him. That's all Patricia knew; nothing about how he died or how long he lived after the heart attack.

Chapter 8

We're Introduced After 25 Years of Marriage

Part of me could hardly wait for the next day, but my skeptical streak held out no expectations. However, I somehow knew that this was going to be a positive experience. I already had faith in Patricia, even though I'd never met her. (We have become great friends in the two years that followed, referring to each other as soul sisters and sharing an incredible bond with each other.) When the time finally came, I was shaking with anticipation. Patricia told me, "I've got Tom here. What do you want to ask him?"

I was so nervous that I couldn't even get my first question out, so Tom just started talking. Through Patricia, he said, "You remember the day I had the heart attack, I awoke in a sweat that morning. I'd had nightmares all night long, and in one of them, I was drowning and could feel the water filling up my lungs. In another, I felt as if I was being suffocated, being buried alive. I couldn't get my breath. And the last dream just before I woke up, I was frantically running away from something hideous, but as hard as I tried, I couldn't seem to escape it. And as I was running, I remember thinking that whatever it was would eventually catch me—that there was nothing I could do."

That hit me hard, because that morning, I awoke to find our bed soaked with sweat. When I questioned Tom, he told me he hadn't slept well, that he had had frightening nightmares and briefly described the details. That amazed me because how could Patricia ever know something that personal? Neither Tom nor I ever talked to anyone else about his nightmares.

Next, Patricia said, "Tom's holding a gray cat. He tells me that its name is Bubba."

I gasped. Holden, our gray Himalayan Persian cat, had died a few years earlier of kidney disease. He'd been extremely obese so Tom and I had affectionately nicknamed him Bubba. Again, my inner skeptic was asking, "How could she have known that?"

For the next hour, I sat on the edge of my seat as she told me things that *only* Tom and I knew. Tom and Patricia just kept the information

flowing, much of it now forgotten because I was in semi-shock throughout the session at the irrefutable stream of evidence for Tom's continued existence. Towards the end of the first session, Patricia was having
trouble receiving something Tom was trying to say, and she asked me,
"Why is Tom wearing a bright red jacket? It looks like a band uniform, a
red blazer. Did he have a jacket like this?"

"Never," I replied. "If you'll pardon the pun, he wouldn't be caught
dead in a red blazer."

A red blazer? And then it hit me and I burst out laughing. "Patricia,
his pride and joy was a candy apple red Chevy Blazer truck."

Even to this day, I can't believe how creative he was with that sym-
bolism, and I often laugh at how it captured his personality so perfectly.
Not only were names, dates and places accurate, but also I was aston-
ished when she repeated verbatim things that only Tom and I shared
during his last hours of life, and even my private, innermost thoughts
that I never even uttered out loud.

Through Patricia, Tom told me, "I heard your thoughts and remembered them."

Tom showed her an image of a photograph of him, and she relayed
a detailed description of it. She also added, "Tom tells me that you talk
to the photo every day and that he thinks that's very sweet. He's telling
me to tell you that he loves you."

Tom also told me, "Just after I died, a beautiful being of light told
me, 'Your wife asked me to carry you home, to help you on this journey
because she knows you're afraid.' "

That was exactly what I had asked for from the deepest recesses of
my soul. There was no way Patricia could have known, unless it really
had come from Tom.

I remember being so emotionally charged during this first reading
that I couldn't control my flood of tears. Yet they were tears of joy and
love. The sadness and loss had begun to dissipate and I finally felt at
peace. As open minded as I had recently become, before this reading,
there still remained a tiny, yet powerful doubt that this was all a result of
the trauma I had experienced in losing him. But as Patricia revealed
such intimate information, the lack of rational alternative explanations
melted my skepticism. And how, I wondered, could she present Tom's
personality as if she had known him all her life, and as if he were in the
room with us.

Patricia passed along Tom's wishes that reminded me of his love for the holidays. He asked me to celebrate in his memory and to set a place for him at the table. He also said he would try to send us a sign to let us know he was with us.

I had invited family and close friends for a small party on Christmas Eve, fifteen people in all. As I waited for people to arrive, I was watching TV, and promptly at six, the time the party was to begin, the TV turned off. I had to chuckle because that was something Tom would do. He was letting me know he was already here.

Later, when we were all eating, celebrating, laughing and having a wonderful time, we couldn't shake the feeling that Tom stood among us, listening and laughing. From time to time, I almost felt him at my elbow, moving with me from person to person. I was having such a joyous time feeling his presence, thinking of him, and being thankful for all the wonderful people in my life.

At one point, I was upstairs in the kitchen when suddenly the lights went out. I found some flashlights and candles and we turned the power failure into a festive occasion. The entire neighborhood, houses, streetlights stood in total darkness, and I thought it odd that we would lose power, especially on such a mild, windless night.

Then someone said, "It's Tom! This is the sign. You told us that Tom promised to send us a sign and he did! This is it!"

"You're right, I agreed. "I can feel him. I know he's here."

Amid the excitement at Tom being with us, we set up candles and talked to him and about him. We all felt his energy and took joy in the reunion. We couldn't see him, but we could *feel* him.

Twenty minutes later, the lights came back on, and so did my skepticism. Maybe it was just a power outage, maybe I "felt" his energy because I so badly wanted to. So, after the holiday, I called the power company and asked, "What happened with the power on Christmas Eve?"

The clerk said, "Oh, yeah. We received several phone calls about that. We sent a crew out but they couldn't find anything wrong. And then the power just came back on."

A chill ran down my spine. "You mean they couldn't find a reason for it?"

"No, ma'am. The transformers and everything checked out fine. The crew couldn't find anything specific so they just put the cause down as 'unknown.' It was the strangest thing. We don't have many outages that turn out that way. Usually they're pretty straightforward—a bad transformer or a line down, but not in this case. It's a real mystery."

Her words finally put most of my skepticism to rest, but more proof was to come.

Just before my second session with Patricia, I put out the thought that I wanted Tom to greet me in a way that I would know, without a doubt, that it was really him. He must have heard my thoughts because the first thing he said was, "Hi, babe, this is your sailor."

I gasped, for this was exactly how he used to greet me whenever he would call me at work. Patricia next said, "Tom is asking me how you liked it when he turned the lights off on Christmas Eve."

Such joy rushed through me! It had really been Tom! As I told her the story, I couldn't help but be proud of him, and thought, "Whoa, he's really good at this."

Tom closed that session with one of the most wonderful messages I ever received through Patricia, one that will forever touch my heart. It was the type of thing he would say to me during his many romantic moods: "You are the breath that I breathe. I am the breath that you breathe. You are the right hand and I am the left. You are in me and I am in you. And we have something no one else has ... each other."

And there was much more to come. Over the next few readings, each further confirmed that Tom was indeed right there in Patricia's office. They were filled with information concerning his journey and more solid details about our life together and the signs he'd been sending. For example, through Patricia, he named my three friends, two of whom were nurses, who had attempted resuscitation before the paramedics arrived. "Please thank them for me." he said.

He spoke about the day of the heart attack, how he was glad that Kathy had taken the pictures of everyone at the cookout, and how he hadn't wanted me to see his stained pants and him without his teeth.

Patricia described him as "speaking extremely fast" and "having much to say," so fast and so talkative, in fact, that she had to move to her computer to type as he spoke since her longhand note-taking couldn't keep up with him. This was good confirmation because Tom had been a very fast talker and always had a lot to say! In fact, we'd given him a tee shirt for his birthday that read, "I'm Talking And I Can't Shut Up!" Again, his true personality had come through with astonishing clarity.

Some skeptics may think that Patricia's staff researches clients to make it look as though she has psychic powers, but readings are conducted with no "cheat sheets" or printed information. And amassing such a volume of information would need a huge staff, which she simply doesn't have.

In the midst of convincing proof of Tom's continued existence, my left-brained ego was doing its best to persuade me that I was losing my grip on reality. Fortunately, Patricia taught me how to rid myself of the fear that presented itself when I was "hearing" his thoughts and to expand my knowledge of meditation to connect with him in a more controlled way. After a while, I began seeing and speaking with him while in an "active" alpha state. During one of these times, I asked him to show me where he lived. I went in and out of the alpha state to write down what I was seeing. Such a beautiful home, surrounded by trees and flowers in colors that we don't even have in the third dimension. Curious to know how accurately I was really receiving, I also asked Patricia to describe where he was living and she described it exactly as I had seen it! So I was beginning to move into his new world. We had definitely begun a new kind of connection and our love was taking on a higher level.

In the months following Tom's death, I fully intended to return to my business career but in the meantime, I wanted to write about my grief experience. I believed that it was of my volition, but Tom told me that *he* was behind the urge to write. And somewhere deep inside, I knew that I would never again reenter the corporate arena.

On the one hand, I was confused, yet on the other hand, I felt more peaceful than I'd ever been. But wait. Wasn't I supposed to be crying and grieving? Noel, my angel guide, brought the answer via a dream. In a gentle yet firm tone told me, "Your life mission has been born out of Tom's death. You have the chance to work, through the Divine Intelligence, to send healing messages to mankind, to re-introduce the subjects of death, dying and the afterlife and to calm those who have become 'weathered by the storm.' "

By means of visions of me writing books, conducting seminars, counseling and working with the dying and their families, Noel showed me what life would be like if I chose to accept this assignment. The dream ended with a warning, "You will need to work hard and continue your studies in order to do this. Peace, my child, cannot be bought. It is complete unto itself, yet only those of 'Light' know how to find it, live in it and pass it along. We ask that you be this child of Light."

So intense was the encounter with Noel that I woke up. Although he had never left my side since the day I became aware of him, I was overwhelmed by his message. How could I carry out such a grand undertaking as this? Didn't he know I wasn't anyone special? I felt unworthy of this work, but in the waking minutes following the dream, something kept pulling me back into it. Every time I tried to escape, more would be shown to me. Eventually, I surrendered, and overwhelmed with intense feelings of love and peace, I decided that I could not turn away from my soul's path. I vowed to keep up the work I had started and to do as much soul-searching as needed to prepare for what was to come.

And at that very moment I saw Tom. And he was smiling.

Chapter 9

Our New Connection

My heart ached for the times I would sit in meditation and be able to "see" into Tom's new world. I was able to connect with Tom at a most profound level, and the closeness of these encounters was fuel for the challenging journey. This was, of course, *all in my mind,* but not in the usual sense. We met between the dimensions, where thoughts were the building blocks of existence, and the only way I could get "there" was through a shift in consciousness. But I was still inside my physical body, aware of everything going on around me, unlike dreaming or astral travel when you tend to forget on awakening.

I also received Tom's thoughts even when I wasn't meditating. It was as if he and I had somehow "blended" in consciousness, somewhere deep inside of me, since I didn't hear him as I would a person outside of myself. Although I shared these awesome experiences with only a few of my closest friends, it didn't matter whether they believed me or thought I was "going off the edge." This was a gift that I was holding on to.

By now, I had finished the "grief" part of my writing, and now Noel suggested I write about death and the afterlife, with Tom assisting me. Noel assured me that I was ready to begin a new technique that Patricia had shown me, what I call "automatic dictation."

I struggled for a while that the source was me rather than Tom, but after some fine-tuning, I was finally satisfied that Tom really was the source of these writings and not my overactive imagination.

After a prayer for protection and some deep breathing, I would slip into a light meditative state, and with me fully awake, pen in hand, the writing would begin. Tom would send his thoughts as usual but with one marked difference. Instead of trying to decipher and analyze the dialogue, I just let my hand go. Many times the words ran together in one long trail. After a few sessions, I switched to the computer because of Tom's habit of talking very quickly. (Now I understood what Patricia meant when she said that she couldn't keep up with him.) So, suddenly, the project had taken on a life of its own.

Tom's material would answer questions I asked and also those he posed. And it didn't matter if I was ready or not. For some reason, the shower seems to be a place where I am most relaxed and Tom knows this, for once in a while, as a joke, he'll come through just as I start to shampoo.

Tom is always a step ahead of me in terms of my research. For instance, although his viewpoint on reincarnation made sense, it differed completely from my understanding. About a week later, however, I found similar viewpoints in several books I had chosen quite by "accident." He also presented me with a very powerful meditation having to do with frequency and sound. Not long after, I found the same technique in a book of ancient eastern meditations. Whatever we talked about, it seemed as if I was led to the corresponding resources. This not only expanded my knowledge, but also increased the credibility of his information.

I believe Tom's role in our writing team is to send uplifting and encouraging insights to a confused, fearful world, with me as the channel. Our main objective is to deliver his material clearly so that mankind can benefit from it.

Tom does not predict my future or influence me to make certain decisions in my life. As with my guides, Tom clearly presents all the options and probable outcomes, allowing me to choose what action to take. Nothing, barring the time of death, is etched in stone and I am free to create and manifest my destiny through the Creative Force, which is a part of me.

The closest Tom ever came to "predicting" an event was in August of 1997. I was meditating with him and became aware that he was embracing my mother. The dull grayish-brown color around her told me that she was very sick. Other than moving more slowly than usual, and with some occasional lightheadedness, she was fairly healthy for her 77 years. I saw her almost every day, so this vision made no sense to me. Tom said that he'd been told that there was disease present and that she needed to be cautious about her health. I began urging her to go to the doctor for a checkup but she assured me that she'd just been and everything was fine. Not wanting to scare her, I let it go but watched her closely. Three weeks later she suffered a sudden, massive heart attack, underwent triple by-pass surgery, and passed away three months later after numerous complications. Tearfully, I "watched" as Tom took her hand and led her into the next dimension of life.

Tom's guidance is often more mundane than spiritual, but just as beneficial. For example, in October of 1996, just six short weeks since his death, I was searching frantically for his gold wedding band which I planned to give to my son, Tommy. I knew that Tom had taken it off the day before his heart attack because we were helping Tommy move to a new apartment, and he didn't want to risk getting it caught while lifting all the boxes. But I couldn't remember where he'd put it. After tearing the house apart for the second time, I sat down, closed my eyes and said, "Okay, Tom, I give up. Where is it?"

He appeared in my mind's eye, grinning from ear to ear. He said nothing but kept reaching into his shirt pocket, and I finally saw that he was reaching for his ring! He must have put it in his shirt pocket and forgotten about it. I rushed to the closet and looked through his shirts. Inside the pocket of the shirt he was wearing the day of the move was his gold wedding band. Somehow, it had survived the washer and dryer.

Another time, I'd cleaned out the bureau to make room for the new bedroom set that would arrive the next day. I called our neighbor who would be taking the old set away in his truck to let him know it was ready. Suddenly Tom said, "Check again!"

I combed every inch of the bureau and found nothing. "Check again," Tom repeated. "Look for the tape."

Thinking he meant an audiotape cassette, I was really puzzled so I sat down, closed my eyes, and tried to concentrate. Tom then showed me an envelope with some writing on it but I couldn't decipher it. Then I got it. I removed all the drawers once more and felt around for something hidden in the body of the bureau. My hand found an envelope taped underneath the top, on which was written "Ireland Trip." In it was almost a thousand dollars in cash! Tom had been secretly saving for the trip we used to talk so much about!

This part of my journey has been the most intensely rewarding. My thirst for knowledge is never satisfied and our dialogues have led me to a greater level of awareness and understanding. The daily enriching energy of Spirit helps carry me through this often discouraging, disappointing physical existence, and has made me aware of myself as a multi-dimensional being while at the same time remaining grounded and centered.

Part Two presents some of the dialogues Tom and I have shared. Some of them come from the sessions with Patricia, but the majority came through me. Please take what resonates with you and add it to your book of truth.

May you find joy and peace on your voyage of Light.

Part Two: Conversations with Tom

Because of you,
I live again.

I passed from the earth
too soon, too fast.

But I've never stopped feeling
the love we shared for so long.

And when I sent you signs of my eternal life,
you listened, and watched, and trusted.

You prayed with me
and for me, and never lost faith.

By the true grace of the Divine,
we enjoy each other's company once again.

Because of your unending belief and love,
I am never empty.

And because of you,
I live again.

— Tom Woods December, 1997

Q. I want to know more about what it's like to die. I'm fascinated not only by the similarities in each NDE case I read about but also by the fact that it all makes such sense. So, Tom, please tell us what the dying process is like.

A. I can only give to you my own experience and what others here have told me. When I first left my body, I was confused as to what had happened. I was watching all that went on at the scene, and when I tried to get back into my body, my energy seemed to "scatter." Part of me was shocked that this could happen at my young age and without warning! I kept going in and out of my body as the paramedics worked to bring me back. I kept trying to embrace you when you cried.

Then I was thrust into a place that was like the tunnel people speak of. I didn't move quickly, but just "floated" on through, filled with an overwhelming sense of love. The tunnel sides were dark but sparkled with what looked like magnificent, sparkling diamonds. Then my guide appeared and said, "My name is Daniel. I know you are shocked about what has happened to you. Your mother and grandparents are here to greet you."

I begged Daniel, "Please don't take me. Let me go back! I'm too young! And I can't leave Walda."

"We sent you signs and tried to warn you but you ignored them all."

I knew what he meant: the dreams of suffocating, of being buried alive and of being chased by something hideous; the small, sharp chest pains I'd felt for about a month before. Looking back, I now see how stubborn I was, and understand the term "free will." I also know now that Daniel was warning me that something was wrong so that I would go to the doctor. Understand that going to the doctor at the first sign of discomfort would have made no difference in terms of my time of death. It was my time to die, something planned long ago as part of my incarnation contract. But I would have found out that I had only weeks to live and would have been able to put some closure to our earth relationship. I needed to tell you so much and felt really short-changed when I died. Your willingness to let me go helped, as did Daniel's assurances that I was not really "leaving" you.

I continued to implore Daniel, "At least let me return long enough to say goodbye."

He agreed, and that was how I suddenly came out of the coma. Even though the respirator prevented me from speaking to you, I knew that you understood that I was only there for a little while longer. It was the cry of your soul that told you, for we were deeply attached to each other. Those last few hours together were necessary for both of us.

Finally Daniel said, "We can't let you stay any longer because your body is shutting down. It's dying." It was then that I heard your thought, "Tom, go into the light. It's okay."

When I finally left my body, I saw a pinpoint of light in the distance, and as I approached it, my fear and confusion left me. As I got closer, I saw some glowing beings and wondered, "Do they have wings?" They didn't; it was their clothing billowing out behind them, along with the beautiful spinning light around them. Then cherubs, like baby angels, smiled at me and said, "Hello, welcome home!"

The light that surrounded me then became me. It was brighter than all the suns that you could experience in a lifetime, and I thought that if I were back on Earth, I couldn't look at it for it would have burned me. Also, I was bathed with indescribable love and ecstasy.

Then, a Being more brilliant than I can describe stood before me but I couldn't see a face. In awe, I kept thinking, "If you are God, then I'm not worthy to be with you right now."

The being must have heard my thoughts, for it said, "You *are* worthy to be with me. Do not be afraid. We are going to make the journey together. Your wife has asked that I help you, to carry you home."

I remembered your belief and thought to myself that if it wasn't for your faith and your belief, God may not have come to me like that.

In a state of indescribable love, I was carried to a place so beautiful that mere human words are inadequate. As I drifted into a sleep state, unseen arms held and rocked me. While in this state of rest, I observed my funeral and heard people saying "good stuff" about me. Then I was back again in the presence of this Being and my angels, and ready to examine my "book of life" which some call the life review. I relived every thought, word and action that had been a part of my life while on Earth.

It's impossible to describe the process or how long it took. It was as if my whole life was one movie that I could see simultaneously. This happened very quickly. I was amazed at how nothing in my life had been hidden. Everything had been recorded in preparation for this very day. I squirmed when asked, "What have you done for your fellow man?" because I was shown the times when I was not very giving, not very loving. Feeling the pain I'd caused and seeing the domino effect it had on others was difficult. At this point, I underwent what you might call a crash course in compassion and tolerance. The lessons I had set up for my life had been arduous and challenging, and to continue my studies in this new existence, I had to admit the wrongs of my life and promise to master the lessons.

I was also shown the good deeds I had accomplished while on Earth, and was proud of the love that I'd given and of the times I'd helped the less fortunate.

My guides also opened up your heart and I could see how much you really loved me. I was also shown our destinies and pre-life agreements. When I saw that we truly are twin souls, I was swept up in a sea of pure bliss. The culmination of this review was being able to feel the passion of the "goodness" part of me, and I vowed to work with others and pass along what I'd already mastered.

I referred to this earlier as like watching a movie but it was so much more than that. This "examination" was filled with vibrant, three-dimensional imagery. And the colors were so brilliant that I remember thinking that I'd never seen colors like this before. I know now that it's not because these colors don't exist while we are in physical form, it's that *our awareness heightens* when the spirit detaches from the physical body. Our perception becomes stronger and we're more able to feel and experience things at a higher level.

I was immediately connected to the Supreme Intelligence, which transformed my three-dimensional thinking into something supernatural, in that I clearly recognized and understood this collection of "life clips" despite the fact that everything was moving so quickly. I was also able to re-live many of the situations, both good and bad, and I could feel the emotions of everyone involved, not just my own. A most powerful emotion swept over me and I wanted to be able to go back and fix all the things I had done wrong. It was at this time that I began to realize the intensity of what was happening to me.

I remember quite vividly that at one point I was watching a scene from my childhood when I was about eight or nine. My younger brother and I were playing outside and he fell down and scraped his face. I picked him up, brought him over to the steps and sat him down. I tried to find a washcloth but finding nothing clean enough to use, I took off my shirt, ran it under cold water and washed his face. I could actually *feel* my brother's sadness fade away, replaced by his intense feeling of comfort.

I was convinced by now that this magnificent light Being was God. He and Daniel kept interjecting through it all, making comments and asking me what I had learned. I was amazed at the gentle way they handled this process. There was no judgment from them at all. I felt their unconditional love for me and I was totally overwhelmed by it. And throughout this review, Daniel was gentle and patient, encouraging me to understand the importance of love.

I also had to be willing to detach from those things of my Earth existence that would keep me earthbound. In a sort of memory erasure, I had to cast aside most of what was in the forefront of my life, such as money, possessions, and yes, even sexual desires, in order to make room for the new attitudes and adjustments of my new world. It was at this time that I saw how much my material worth meant to me. Instead of seeing my possessions as "life tools," I had become a slave to them. I wasn't greedy, but money was certainly a main focus for me. When I lost my job, I couldn't think of anything worse that could have happened. I didn't realize then that financial security, a house, trips and shiny new cars are not the most important part of life. I now know that only love is real. Nothing else exists. It is the life force of the universe, the only thing you can freely give away and never run out of. And it's the only thing you're allowed to bring into the next world.

Some may think that when you die, you become all-knowing. This is not so, although many Universal Truths *are* revealed at this time, truths that the soul has known from the beginning of its existence but have laid dormant in the soul's recesses.

I guess the biggest surprise I had was that, when we die, we are not judged by an angry God! We judge ourselves, using the Universal Mind, the part of us that is the Divine Source. Our soul and spirit are made up of energy and the vibration of this energy consists of the good and bad that we have done on Earth. It determines the level in our new world with which we most resonate.

With Daniel beside me and through the universal mind of the Source, I was allowed to use the power of thought to "create" where I would live—my home, the mountains, the flowers, and so on.

From those I have talked with here, these are typically the stages of dying but each is unique and some occur in a different order. I would continue, but I know you will ask more of me later on these subjects, so I'll close for now.

Q. Learning about the afterlife is intriguing but I want to know more about these new dimensions. The term "where" gets in the way of my progress, so let me ask you, "Where is the 'afterlife'?"

A. The afterlife dimensions are not "places" in any earthly sense that you can go to in a car or a boat or even a spaceship, although some of your cults would argue the part about the spaceship. They are non-physical dimensions and exist beyond your five senses. They consist of interwoven levels of energy and consciousness that intermingle with your plane but vibrate at a much higher frequency. The simplest way for me to explain this is to compare these dimensions to radio stations. They each broadcast on a particular frequency, and just because you're listening to one radio station doesn't mean that the other stations aren't broadcasting. You just happen to be tuned into one particular station. You on Earth are "tuned into" the physical dimension. Because you cannot discern us with your physical senses does not mean that we don't exist. We simply occupy another frequency band, and are in and around your physical plane.

Another example is the household fan. Once it's turned on, the rapid movement of the blades seems to make them disappear, but this is only because your perception can no longer follow the frequency (speed) of the blades. They still exist but you can no longer see them. They change frequency, that's all.

When the physical body can no longer sustain life, it dies and the energy that makes up the soul and spirit continue on, in a state of consciousness that is eternal. Remember, the soul houses the body, and not the other way around.

Man was created in physical form to learn the concept of separateness. Dying is simply a matter of changing frequency! Having an out-of-body experience while still alive on Earth is similar, only the "silver cord" of which many speak is not severed, allowing the astral consciousness to return to the body.

Here we do not age because our frequency is higher and close to the frequency of thought. It is through thought that we determine our appearance. The concept of time in our world is probably the most difficult to speak about because the time and space we "experience" here do not have physical attributes. They are continuums that have no beginning or end, so to try to describe it to you is difficult because you cannot comprehend anything outside of your physical experience. For example, your linear time is clocked by the earth's rotation in terms of seconds, minutes, and hours. Time is a necessary tool in the physical world and it defines your existence. However, without getting into an advanced phys-ics lesson, I will attempt the near impossible.

There is only the eternal now moment and nothing else in relation to time exists. Everything is happening NOW, even the past! If it were not for memory, the past would not exist! The fact is that the only way you can remember the past is to think about it through memory in the NOW moment. When it *did* happen, it was in the present NOW mo-ment.

The same goes for the future. The future hasn't happened yet and the only way you can relate to the future is to think about it through expectation in the NOW moment. When it *does* happen, it will be the present NOW moment. The real question is, where does the past end and the present begin? And where do the present end and the future begin? The answer is NOW. Because we live in a more spacious NOW, we here can perceive events across the timeline as if they are all happen-ing at once, without becoming overwhelmed.

The world in which I live is more real to me than where you are is to you. Without your five senses, none of what you have there would exist. That makes your reality a realm of illusion, I would guess. Yours is the densest of all dimensions, "vibrating" at a very slow speed. Here, every-thing is light and unrestricted, and we create from the pure energy of our thoughtforms. The vibrations are extremely high, and get higher still as we progress to the higher dimensions beyond. Some of you are able to catch glimpses of our world through meditation, for in the medi-tative state, your frequency increases and your awareness heightens.

When you are sleeping, you drop into a lower state of conscious activity, your frequency rises, and the spirit frees itself from its physical anchor. Now, during sleep, your conscious awareness is usually dormant, and has no idea what your spirit, or Higher Self is doing, but sometimes you can remain partially aware, and you experience your Higher Self's activities as a dream. So, your dreams present you with one of the best examples of the freedom you have to create on our side.

In actuality, you "die" every night when you go to sleep! Sleep is actually the spirit leaving the body for a brief vacation. In fact, it usually needs the much-deserved rest more than your physical body does. Your spirit may hover just over the body in its astral state or it may travel. It is then that the spirit can enter our world for lessons with its guides and to visit deceased friends and loved ones. So when you sometimes dream of them, you are actually paying them a nocturnal visit.

Few can recall these events because, I'm told, remembering the ecstasy and joy of our world would cause your physical body to want to die in order to come here. Have you noticed that those who've had NDEs say that they didn't want to come back to their earthly lives?

In meditation and dreams, you get mere mental glimpses into our dimensions, so as an observer, you do not get the full "treatment," and can return. There is almost always recall of this. You yourself, Walda, often cross the bridge between worlds during meditation.

If I have rambled, it's only because I'm trying to give you a linear account of a totally non-linear environment in which everything seems to relate to everything else.

Q. I'm curious about the different levels/dimensions of your new existence. I have investigated many resources, all of which seem to give similar explanations. What's your account?

A. The first level is the lowest, with which murderers, rapists and other heinous figures resonate. They will stay there until they realize their oneness with the Source, learn their lessons and choose to move on. They always have the help of their guides and angels who occasionally "feed" them some of the light from the higher dimensions. Many would probably call this area *hell* or *purgatory* but it's not hot as many may think. It's actually very cold and gloomy in comparison to the higher levels. It may take thousands of years for a spirit to move out and upward but eventually everyone has this chance. So eternal hell only happens if one chooses it. There is much suffering in this dimension, but there is also a great deal of help and support.

The second level is for suicides, traumatic and sudden deaths, prolonged illness and the like. It is here that they receive special attention to help them to adjust to their new surroundings. Some even refuse to believe that they have died! There are hospitals where the spirit is cleansed and nurtured, loved and comforted by helpers who devote their time here to assist others. Most stay for just a short time for the rest and care, and then go on to review their "book of life." I spent some time here and remember how wonderful it was to wake up in this place and see a smiling face welcoming me home. A spirit may stay on this level even after the assigned rest period. It is here that they create their home and surroundings while attaining the consciousness necessary to move to the next level.

Suicides, however, are a different story. There is a special area for those who consciously interrupt their life cycle. Their energy is "scattered," as they find that death is not at all what they had expected. They were hoping for an escape but here, they realize that they have brought all of their old problems into their new existence, the only difference being that they no longer have a physical body. Everything else is the same.

Suicides also become aware of the pain and suffering they caused those left behind. This is so traumatic for them that they need more time to rejuvenate before they go on to the next step. Always there are helpers and angels to assist, and no one is ever alone. However, the emotional pain suffered after suicide surpasses the anguish that caused them to commit this act. Though prayers are always helpful to the departed, it is especially important to pray for the suicides. Your prayers fill them with love and keep them spiritually connected to you. *Mankind must understand that suicide is never an option.* But you must also understand that these spirits, too, are embraced and when they are ready to move on, they will.

The third level is where most people go (including me) either directly after death or after their period of "rest." Many come here looking for God on his throne and angels, harps and the like. They think they are going to spend eternity floating around on a cloud! What they actually find is the many opportunities for soul growth, great love for the Source, and a true sense of brotherhood. We feel unity with every flower, rock, bird, and animal, and there is a kinship between all things, because we *are* one with all things.

I know this sort of language must seem strange coming from me, but the experience of Divine Love has brought me to the level I am now, and allows me to see the beauty of all that is here. There is no pain or suffering, jealousy or selfishness. Although we can and do feel your sadness when you mourn, it's not as we felt it when on Earth. It's just pure compassion.

Religion here means nothing and we are reminded that the most important thing Jesus taught was unconditional love. Period. If you don't practice this teaching while on Earth, then all the religion in the world doesn't matter!

Beautiful meadows, mountains, oceans, forests and landscapes surround us. The flowers are brilliant with colors that do not exist on Earth. Everything is vibrant and nothing is ever neglected. Nothing evil can exist, as all evil is immediately transformed into light.

We all have our interests and activities, and plenty of schools of learning, libraries and museums. The light is so magnificent that the longer we are here, the more intense the vision and feeling in our soul to seek the way to higher dimensions. As a result, we are all encouraged to choose a mission or service, and carry it out eagerly and happily, such as hospital work, committees and study groups for the betterment of mankind, and assisting the more timid spirits in "crossing over." The arts are highly regarded here and musicians are in abundance and greatly appreciated. Our guides here continue to guide, direct and teach us. We are constantly meeting and sharing, but most importantly, we learn continuously.

There are no conditions here. We are able to do just about anything—ride a dolphin, climb a mountain, and play golf. We are not limited as you are in your world. As far as eating is concerned, we do not need to eat because we have no bodily organs. Hunger, as we knew it while on Earth, does not exist. But food is still available if the pleasure of eating is desired. (We create whatever we want, and no, we don't have to watch our weight!) But after a while, the "desires of the earth" fade away, making room for more spiritual aspirations. The intent is always toward a higher consciousness.

Regarding sleep, again, because we have no bodily organs, we do not have a physical need for sleep. We do have a spiritual need for meditation and sitting in the silence, which creates the soul consciousness that is necessary for our learning and growth.

There are "churches" of a sort but they are more assemblies of devotion where we meditate and pray. It is also here that the prayers you send us are received and heard. Once more, let me assure readers that your prayers help our progress and fill us with happiness.

We have astral bodies that match our physical bodies but they are really not necessary considering the fact that everything is done telepathically here and that the essence of one's spirit is felt and recognized. You will be interested to know that the astral body rejuvenates itself when the physical body dies, so amputees regain their limbs, cancer patients have their hair, etc., and the spirit is once again whole.

When I first arrived, I worried that I wouldn't understand someone from a foreign country but when they speak, it's as if a translation button is pushed! Using our one universal language, I have had many wonderful conversations with great people of other cultures and am grateful because this is something I always wanted to do while on Earth. I never believed that one's skin color, heritage or culture determine a man's worth, and have been blessed here to see these truths in action. This must seem so far-fetched coming from me, since I was prone to generalize about certain races. Even though I did this without malice, I feel this ignorance may have come from my upbringing. As a self-taught man, since childhood, I always yearned to communicate with other races but couldn't because of the language barrier.

The light here is radiant and with each "leap" to the next dimension, we become brighter and brighter because we are closer to the Source. Our sense of learning is enhanced because we are increasingly able to tap into Universal Intelligence. When I read a book, I don't have to worry about remembering or retaining; I just read it and I know it!

Here, thought is a powerful tool, and the source of all that's in our world. Manifestation here is respected and never abused. The beauty of a rose captivates us much more than piles of money or other material things. Talking of natural beauty, birds ride on cats' backs, dogs and squirrels romp and play, all with no animalistic tendencies or anger.

Everything here is done through thought, or telepathy. If we want to be somewhere or with someone, we just think of that person or place and we are instantly there, including coming in and out of the Earth plane. We can visit the lower levels, but those on the lower levels cannot enter the higher realms until they have achieved a higher state of awareness. Then, of course, their enhanced frequency will naturally elevate them to a higher level of existence. In our world, frequency levels operate precisely, and our conscious awareness is what allows us to "fit" into a certain dimension. And until the time comes to move upward, we must be patient and work hard. I have joked with Daniel that this is "God's incentive plan."

We have free will just like we had on Earth. We don't do anything with which we're uncomfortable, and no one ever falls from grace. So if people tell you not to summon us or disturb us, tell them that if we didn't want to be bothered, we simply wouldn't respond. The deep love we share with those of you on Earth brings us close to you and it must be mutual.

The fourth level is for further development of the soul. Study groups meet to discuss art, inventions, music, poetry, writing and discoveries, which in turn are passed on to receptive minds on Earth. The term "inspiration" comes from the Latin words for "into" and "breathe," so we literally breathe new ideas into you.

Because of the work that you and I are doing, I was able to move to this new level much more quickly than most, and can now move back and forth to the earth plane with ease. I am also able to be with you much more now, spiritually, even when we're not meditating together. I have blended my consciousness with yours—my thinking and yours have become one, making it easier to connect and share. Because we have chosen to do this work together, you are able to sit down and write our blended thoughts on these pages. Many of the world's famous composers, writers, artists, philosophers, doctors and so on have done this and will continue to do this, the overarching objective being progress toward enlightenment.

It is on this level that the spirit becomes more philosophical, but do not fear, for the "down to earth" part will always remain. There is a greater understanding of Universal Truths and the Light here is magnificent. It is here that we begin a detachment from any type of "body," astral or otherwise. We become "light beings" and recognize one another through pure essence of spirit. The idea of separateness has no meaning and the concept of "group soul" is understood.

The levels five through ten are known as the Celestial Kingdoms. These planes are beyond earthly comprehension and even I'm not completely aware of them as yet. Not being able to visit them freely, I must rely on what Daniel and my teachers tell me. The tenth level consists of superior wisdom and understanding, and is home to pure Light Beings who have "completed" their cycle of earthly lives. Perfected expression and unity with the Source is the climax of this ascension. They have a complete connection with All That Is, and some go on to serve as guides. The masters, gurus, sages and saints exist in these dimensions. Your readers can find many great books on this subject channeled from the ascended consciousness.

Q. I have just finished my hospice training and there's been much discussion about "death bed visions" and how a person reacts just before death. Can you tell me more?

A. When a person is close to death, all the significant entities, such as their deceased loved ones, angels and guides are informed and wait, ready to greet the new arrival. Because the dying are in between levels of consciousness, they frequently see these beings. They will extend a hand or embrace the one who is dying saying, "It's all right. Come on now. It's time to go."

So many are fearful of letting go, even in a comatose state, that this is very comforting for them. Sometimes visiting relatives also see us, but most of the time, it's just the dying person who gets a glimpse. It's also possible for the dying to see flashes of our world, but these visions are often dismissed, especially by the medical profession, as hallucinations—the result of a dying brain deprived of oxygen, or maybe all the drugs that have been given. However, a dying person often sees a vision of someone he doesn't even know has died because the family has chosen not to tell him. And why do these "hallucinations" most usually happen right before death, and not at other times?

A hospice nurse here with us witnessed many passings while there on Earth. She tells us that she often saw what she calls the "angel of death," and knew that the patient's time was near. A dedicated and caring professional, she was not what you in your world would call crazy or fanciful. She now knows that what she saw was real.

As for how a person reacts right before death, even now I am amazed at the stories people here have told me. Firstly, we do not want you to see us take our last breath. We don't want that to be your last memory of us, so we try to hang on until you leave the room. Your Mom wants to remind you that you stayed with her for many hours after life support had been disconnected. She clung to life for a long time, but when she was finally ready, she worried about you having to see her die. So when you finally left the room to stretch your legs, she took that opportunity to leave.

Sometimes a person will wait to see someone they love before they die. Or wait to see a specific event such as the birth of a child. Then there are those who are so fearful that they just hang on and hang on. Or they may feel that you don't want them to go, even with all the coaxing and comforting going on from over here!

Please tell your readers that it is sometimes necessary to tell the person, as you did, "It's okay. We'll be all right. Go on, now. Go into the Light. You have our permission."

This is hard to do, but essential to a peaceful death. So you see, the dying have a little control during this most vulnerable time.

There are some dedicated ones on Earth who are bringing something called "deathing" into the folds. Much like "birthing," it is a preparation for the dying process. The process includes techniques for before, during and after death. Look for a book on this and more to come. It will revolutionize how the Western world views the dying process and will emphasize peaceful death.[1]

Q. Wanting to know what life is like after the transition, and having read extensively on this subject already, I have a lot of unanswered questions. Can you tell us more about the life of spirit?

A. Spirit is an extremely sensitive, high frequency energy. The pure creative thought energy of the mind survives death, leaving the physical plane and moving to the higher dimensions. This life force—the stuff we were created with and from—never dies.

Let me clarify the difference between the mind and the brain. The brain is a physical organ and does not survive death. It is the tangible (physical) vehicle for the intangible (non-physical) mind. The mind holds the everlasting consciousness energy, and cannot be measured with your scientific devices.

In view of our refined composition, we can "activate" things from where we are because there really is no here and there, just different frequencies. This creates the paranormal occurrences you so often refer to as "spirit communication" from our world. You must understand that spirit is often around you and you should not ignore feelings and signs of our presence. Since coming here, I have spoken to many new arrivals, and they all say the same thing: that directly after death, they yearn to see their loved ones once again. Because thought is so powerful here, we think it and instantly we are with you, trying to convince you that we are not really gone! In our eagerness to tell you about our new life, we are often frustrated at your inability to see, hear or feel us. We want you to know we are safe and that what exists after the death of the physical body is far from just cold, dark earth! So if you visit a cemetery, please do not think of us lying in the ground. In fact, we probably have our arms around you, consoling you in your grief.

Death is much like birth, and gives the spirit the chance for a new beginning. Rejoice and know that we are well taken care of. And remember first and foremost—the one way to always stay connected is through love, for it is love that joins our respective existences. It will be that love that enables mankind to communicate with the deceased. If there is no love, true contact will never be made.

Sometimes, when you call for us, it may seem as if we don't answer. Now, we can be with you in the blink of an eye if need be, and by something called transference of energy, we can also be in many places at once. So know that our presence is with you when you call, even though you may not notice the clues we present you with.

Many times, my woman, you called out for me to send a sign to prove that I was in the room with you, and I tried, I really did, but nothing happened. I don't know why that is. Other times, our energy comes barreling through in strong bursts and you recognize it clearly. It is then that we celebrate, because we are happiest when our loved ones are joyful! The longer we are in this world of Love and Light, the stronger our energy becomes.

After a while, we gain a better perception of why we're here and why things happened the way they did. So, as we move ahead in our progression, the familiar "signs" become less frequent. It is also time for those left behind to move forward in their progression. Communication or connection can still take place, but will be accomplished more through meditation and thought transference between human and Spirit, and less through "demonstrations."

On this subject, never underestimate the spiritual insight of children! Children under the age of five are still extremely close to the world of spirit from whence they only recently came. Their "third eye," meaning the psychic or sixth-sense, has not yet closed, although societal programming will eventually shut it down. Children are very open to spirit and can feel and see this energy in the form of apparitions, hence the frequent invisible companions. Angels play and romp with them, occasionally holding a finger to their lips as if to say, "Shhh," in anticipation of being discovered! The deceased visit the young quite often and bring words of comfort and a soothing touch. Babies sometimes laugh in their sleep, usually indicating an excursion to other dimensions where they are joyfully welcomed and entertained during "dream time."

Children may often stare off into space as if under a hypnotic "spell." In fact, they're actually in the alpha meditative state, which they move in and out of quite easily. Their connection with our world is intense and focused, which is why they sleep so much during their early years. The spirit takes its time in adjusting to being part of a body and sleep is the "comfort zone" of the transition to human form, or "break time" if you will.

The spirits that we are most concerned about are those earthbound spirits that do not successfully make the transition to the next plane of existence. After they leave their physical bodies, they stay behind, cruising their familiar haunts, refusing to give up old habits and sometimes making a nuisance of themselves. Angels, guides and helpers try to assist those stuck in between "here and there," but unless the stragglers choose to move forward, no one can force them. So the angels stay close, coaxing, urging and comforting. Sometimes, religious exorcism may be necessary to push them along. There are also some caring souls on Earth— mediums and spiritualists—who intervene if they can, and your prayers always help.

If one of these "ghosts" visits you, simply tell it to look for the Light and go towards it. Do not exhibit fear, for fear fuels these entities. Instead, acknowledge and call upon the love of the Source, and eventually these lost spirits will wander freely into our world and wonder why they didn't come sooner!

Q. Tom, what's a typical day like on the other side?

A. As you know, there's no linear time here, so to describe a typical "day" is not possible for me. But I can give you an idea of what fills our existence here.

There are different levels of this new world, each level providing opportunities for growth to the higher dimensions, and this is what we're constantly striving for. We often meet with our teachers and guides because we are continually learning how to better ourselves. They suggest missions and lessons for us and are available when we have questions. The masters here teach a higher awareness and encourage us to carry out whatever is necessary for enlightenment. There are also many meetings with the Council of Light to determine the parameters for the next incarnation.

We have infinite learning resources from which to draw. Some people take up where they left off during their Earth life, and others decide to become proficient in things they always wanted to master but couldn't. The learning process is much different, though, since we connect with Universal Mind and are instantly aware of what we have just read or been given in our lectures.

Meditation occupies much of our time, since it's here that we become one with the Source and see the beauty in the stillness. Just as you use sleep, we use this time to "re-fuel" as well as maintain our energy level, since unity with the Source brings us to higher levels of consciousness. Sometimes I sit and listen to the waterfall behind my house. After a while, I become a *part* of the waterfall, which helps me to understand the miracle that is Divine Intelligence.

As I mentioned earlier, most of us choose a mission or missions such as hospital work, assisting the "crossing over" of timid spirits, and helping others to adjust to their new surroundings. We also have the opportunity to work with people in the Earth plane to carry out their lofty goals. Many committees and study groups on our side work toward the betterment of mankind. Art, inventions, music, poetry, writing and discoveries are discussed in these groups and passed on to receptive minds in the earth.

We also devote ample time to relaxation and fun, such as mountain climbing, swimming, motorcycling, playing golf or just sitting in a beautiful garden. There are no limits or danger of any kind so we are free to try "dangerous" things we never could while in our physical bodies.

As you see, we're very busy here, so forget any notion of floating around all day on a cloud.

Q. How does one's beliefs of the afterlife affect his/her transition?

A. Let me start by saying that whatever religious views you have will directly affect the perception of who and what you see when you first arrive. For instance, a Catholic may see one of the saints or even the Virgin Mary; a Buddhist may see Buddha; a Christian will see Christ; a Jew may find himself in a beautiful synagogue; a Baptist could experience a gospel service. This is all due to your programmed beliefs and what you are most comfortable with. Children will almost always see their guardian angels.

Expecting angels, harps and clouds, many new arrivals are truly disappointed. At first, they refuse to believe they have died! It takes a lot of patience on the part of the spirit helpers and guides to convince them.

Those who were taught to fear the Creator fully expect to see an angry God on his throne, shaking his fist in judgment, so the life review is sometimes difficult for them because they think they're being duped. Judgment Day has arrived and they can't believe that the process is filled with so much love and compassion instead of guilt and damnation. Those who led a moral but austere life in which they did little to help their fellow man may arrive expecting their piety to be rewarded, but instead re-experience how their spiritual arrogance hurt other people.

Arrivals who do not believe in any type of afterlife expect nothingness, so they sleep a while. Every time they wake up, they're greeted with a smile and a gentle touch. Fearful of where they are, they slip back into a state of rest. Special spirit healers are brought in to help, but until the new arrivals come to terms with their new existence, they remain in this state.

Those who believe they have sinned against the Church expect to spend eternity in the fires of hell, so that is what they create for themselves. Because they cannot seem to get past this conception, their life review is continually postponed. At some point, they agree to accompany their guides and begin this process. Once they feel the glow of warmth and unconditional love, they began to understand exactly what's going on and that their prior beliefs were not truth.

Those with the most solid perception, through faith, of what the afterlife will be like have the most peaceful transition. During life, spirituality and death education are vital in order to ensure the easiest passage in the early stages. It also helps if you pray for the deceased, especially if they have no preconceived ideas about their new existence.

Q. Please explain about the soul's choices before birth.

A. Before the soul incarnates, its master guides and Council of Light Beings assist it in determining the lessons necessary for further development, and putting together the best scenario for learning them. What has already been accomplished during previous lives has much to do with this. All previous incarnations are present during these meetings and the process is precisely orchestrated. The input and contributions by each incarnation are critical for planning the next "blueprint." The exquisite joy of being in the presence of your "soul family" is beyond description, and is intensely emotional, even for us here. It's as if you already know each one intimately. Because of the cellular memory contained in each spirit, when you meet them, you have instant recall of all previous lifetimes, full understanding of the All That Is and that *we are all one.* I remember also being in awe of my own soul or God-self, with deep reverence for this "creator behind the creator."

Additional angels and guides are chosen according to what needs to be achieved. A plan of sorts is drawn up but, as you know, nothing, except for the time of death, is etched in stone. Because of free will, decisions can be changed and circumstances altered. The only thing that is predetermined is when death of the physical body will occur. Although it is not always predestined how you will die, you will return "home" when the time comes that your soul has previously chosen, whether or not you have accomplished all that you set out to do in that particular incarnation.

Depending on what needs to be completed, a prolonged death or a sudden death is chosen. This is chosen to maximize the benefit of all concerned: you and the others you have "contracted" with. Nothing is wasted, with everything that happens offering opportunities to learn and grow, and death is no exception. Someone dying of AIDS, for example, could be an old soul who opted to incarnate for the purpose of his means of death helping his family understand and master unconditional love. A young mother who loses her husband suddenly in a tragic car accident could be attempting to learn faith. Or in dealing with his death, she is able to help others to overcome their grief.

Everything you do starts out with a desire from your soul and all thoughts and actions are connected to your life plan. The purpose of your life is to satisfy your soul's balance (or karma as some call it), which is not punishment, but rather a balancing that enables you to experience what you need to master. So you are on Earth to satisfy the balance between your soul and those of others, and undergo experiences initiated by you and others, both intentional and non-intentional. The flow is eternal and continuous, and the plan is well thought out and in perfect harmony with all issues. This may sound to you to be a monumental yet tedious task, but understand that all of this is done through the Universal Mind. The greatest minds on Earth could not accomplish this with the perfection it calls for. In conversation with Daniel, I decided to call it the "Divine Computer."

Once this soul outline is in place and conception has taken place in the womb, nothing can interfere with its progress, not even the Source itself. Remember, the Divine is *within you,* and no one can intercede in the situations and experiences that you have chosen both before birth and after. This is the pact between the Source and its creations, our souls. Guidance and direction by Spirit can be heeded or ignored, but nothing can be forced upon you. The perfected state is the goal of all spirits working for the soul, and this task is undertaken with total conviction.

When I say that everything that happens to you on Earth is caused entirely by you and no one else, some readers may feel that I'm being cold. The truth is that many people are so quick to assign blame for the events in their lives to "circumstances beyond their control" and thereby duck personal responsibility. Just know that at some point in time, either consciously or unconsciously, you chose to be where you are, doing what you're doing.

As I said earlier, you must each master the assignments you built into your pre-life plan. You set these lessons up to learn from in order for you to remember who you really are and to experience *being* divine love. Again, every one of you incarnates with a life purpose, or mission, and while you may be ambitious in setting up challenges to accelerate your growth, your journey does not have to be filled with suffering and hardship! Your Higher Self (or soul or Godself) is naturally playful and joyful, so if you are in loving connection with it, your path will always be joyful. This is why prayer and meditation are such wonderful tools. They are your direct connections to your Higher Self, where the answers to all your questions lay. They are also the tools for creation and manifestation in your life. All the direction, guidance and help you need are there. When you reach a crossroad and don't know which way to turn, ask! But ask, "Which path is best for my soul's journey?" Ask to be placed in whatever situations best enhance your spiritual progress. The road may have trials and tribulations but there are also triumphs and victories. Embrace them all and know that you are on a journey of light. And never forget that the real you is spirit, your soul, and not a physical body.

Q. My studies have revealed much evidence of past lives, but I'm worried that you might reincarnate before I get there. Would you explain the process, please?

A. The terms "soul" and "spirit" are sometimes used interchangeably, but they are very different.

The soul has many names, among them Higher Self, God-Self, and Inner Self. It is eternal, and undertakes a cycle of thousands of Earth lifetimes, each time with a well thought out plan. This is what is known as re-incarnation. The Source or All That Is created souls, just as a river contains many droplets of water. Each drop is made up of "river stuff" but is separate unto itself, holding all the answers that its physical incarnations desperately seek.

This brings me to a question I know you'll ask sooner or later. "Why was I created? Why am I here?"

When I came to my new world, I wanted to know the reason for life. What was this all about, anyway? If the soul already knows everything, what kind of game was this? And why bother? Fortunately, the longer I was here, the clearer the answer became.

In each lifetime, the incarnating consciousness, or spirit, is born with "amnesia," in that it doesn't know who or what it really is, and the soul constantly strives to have it remember. But simply knowing all the answers is not enough. The real goal is to encounter and experience Love and Light, and to hence BE Love and Light. The soul accomplishes this through the spirit, as the spirit is the soul's way of forgetting. The joy comes when the spirit, knowing quite well what it feels like to forget, finally "wakes up" and realizes who it really IS. This dichotomy of human life is intended to bring a soul to the joyful experience of remembering what it is like to truly BE. As I said before, this will be achieved through the experiences of thousands of Earth incarnations. We are all God, manifested and incarnated into physical existence in order to experience BEING.

And now to define spirit. The spirit could be defined as a "piece" of the soul with which the soul imbues each incarnation. The soul, therefore, consists of many different "pieces" or *spirits* from its various incarnations. *In simple terms*, the soul defines the parameters for a new incarnation, and then "delegates" part of itself to be intimately associated with and "manage" the incarnation.

The spirit body, the astral body (or emotional body), the mental body (or mind), and the physical body make up the incarnation while on Earth. After death, the physical body is left behind, but the other three bodies merge (except in the case of haunting) and move to a higher dimension, although not always on the same level as the soul. Having had the physical body as an "anchor" for a time, these three bodies now work in perfect harmony as one body. The restrictions of the physical body are no longer present and this new "body of bodies" now works effortlessly as one.

All of the "soul pieces" will eventually reach perfection and merge back with the soul, which will no longer need to incarnate. The blended soul and its pieces will then exist in a highly evolved state of consciousness and perfect unity with the Source, which, I am told, is such pure ecstasy that even we here cannot imagine it until we experience it.

For you on Earth, your soul retains all of the memories of its past lives and these are recorded in each spirit incarnation's cellular memory. This is accessible to your consciousness in the form of dreams, déjà vu, and so on. Or they may surface during past life recall under hypnotherapy.

Now, you are worried that I may have already reincarnated when you arrive here, and that I won't be here to greet you. Please be assured that it is not "I" who will reincarnate, and I will be waiting for you for a grand reunion. Of course, my soul will continue its inexorable journey toward perfection, and may well have "delegated" other sparks of itself into other incarnations. But the soul spark you know as Tom will be here, waiting. Please pass this vital piece of information on to your students and readers. [2]

Q. Can you clarify karma? I perceive it as a punishment yet I'm trying to reconcile this with the fact that the Source consists of loving energy.

A. The true concept of karma is not what most people have been taught. For so long, karma has been thought of in terms of punishment and this is simply not true. Karma is the law of cause and effect, although we here call it the soul's balance. It has to do with the choices you make and how you decide to live your life.

For every action, there is a re-action. For example, if a person is very greedy with his possessions and watches his relatives or friends suffer without food and shelter, and does not attempt to help them during his lifetime, in another lifetime (not necessarily the next), he may be extremely poor and lacking love from his family and friends. He now feels the hurt that he caused in not extending a hand to his "brothers," and he also experiences the absence of love.

Now, you may interpret this suffering as punishment but it is far from that! It is the soul's way of experiencing both sides of the situation: to be in need and to deny succor to those in need. And it all comes down to all the different ways to experience love. For until you live a loveless life and really know what it's like to *be without love*, you cannot truly *be* love. You can know *about* it in every sense of the word. You see, love is a constant flow of energy, a give and take, and until all aspects are mastered, the soul will continue to experience what is necessary to realize what it is to BE pure love and light.

What I am about to tell you may seem harsh to some but please know it as truth: You already know that everything in the universe is connected through the energy of the All That Is. It is continual motion, ever-changing. (In fact, the only thing that never changes is the fact that everything is always changing!) For example, a man is suffering from a terminal illness that is part of his soul balance in this lifetime. His wife watches him suffer and feels his torment, and also must experience losing him through death. As part of her soul's evolution, she needs to explore compassion, forgiveness and respect for human life. Hopefully, she may choose, at some point, to apply what she learns in service to mankind, assisting others to better understand life and death, and, most importantly, to turn her pain into joy, both for herself and for others. Only then will she have mastered the assignment. Such mastery may be gained in one lifetime or several, but the soul will ensure that every facet of the lesson is well learned.

Tell your readers that life presents many choices, and that each one has consequences. The soul's intent is to gear all choices to creating joy for itself, for this ultimately creates joy for others. Do not allow the self to become an assortment of reflexive conditionings that only react to certain stimuli. You must take control of the situations at hand and know that life is a great tapestry of countless millions of interwoven threads. And the finished picture? Love.

Q. For a long time, I have been searching for the meaning of organized religion. In terms of death and the afterlife, the religious texts seem to leave too many questions unanswered. Also, they teach a fearful picture of Heaven and Hell. Many who attend my seminars are experiencing similar difficulties. So why is the church so reluctant to speak about the afterlife?

A. The Church is not equipped to deal with grief and bereavement. At one time, the gifts of prophecy and wisdom of discerning spirits were an everyday part of religion, but this came to an abrupt halt when the major religions decided that, by allowing their followers to look outside the standard texts for their answers to life and death, they were giving away too much power and, of course, revenue, both of which the Church needed to survive.

Religion *should* teach that people are responsible for their thoughts, words and actions—this is what will determine how and where they will live when they enter the next world. Instead, the clergy preaches fire and brimstone, hell and fury, judgment and punishment from an angry God as a means of control. My all time favorite is that if you are not a member of a particular church, the gates of Heaven will be closed to you! Now, I ask you, does that make sense? By equating death with torment and eternal damnation, no wonder most people are afraid of dying. This deeply saddens us.

Most Christian sects label spirit communication as the work of the devil. Visions and signs are reserved for the "holy," not the normal folk. And if followers do comfort themselves with spiritual practices that bring much needed peace, the elders of their religious order will denounce them, even expel them.

Major western religions do not, as a rule, have any satisfying answers for the grieving. Tissue thin quotes such as, "It was God's will" leave those who are saddened with more questions. This forces them to see the Divine Source as an angry, judgmental being who randomly chooses who lives and who dies. Not being rooted in love, this creates more fear.

While organized religion is a source of comfort and faith for many, there will come a time when mankind will turn away from the rigid teachings and more toward the Inner Light that shines within all of us. The Source is pure love, and anything expressed otherwise is not of the Light.

Q. How can we begin to live spiritually?

A. One word: Commitment. A total dedication to living with Spirit. Your commitment to your own spirituality will bring incredible peace to your life that you can draw from any time you need it. It is part of the human condition that sudden, unannounced tragedy can disrupt your life. Also, most of you live under constant, low level stress, such as the threat of unemployment, financial problems, and tensions at home. Unfortunately, most of you do not begin to explore spirituality until you are just about on the edge and ready to crack. It is then that your spirit uses the crisis to cry out for a new direction as it did when we both lost our jobs.

Why wait until things fall apart to discover a new and fulfilling life? For this is when we here rejoice in the rapture of your discovery.

What exactly does spirituality mean? To be spiritual is to live in constant awareness of your spirit and soul, to know them in a very intimate and personal way, and to understanding that the Divine is part of you and you are part of the Divine.

Those who are spiritual know that there's no such thing as coincidence, that synchronicity travels with you every day, and that some things are beyond rational understanding. Spirituality means living with spirit, knowing that you do not walk alone, that even those who have gone on before are with you, bound by the love that you still share even after physical death. It means accepting that your angels and guides are assisting you and "speak" to you all the time. You stop asking why things happen and begin to focus on dealing with the issues at hand. You acknowledge the many miracles of this journey.

Through meditation, you explore the inner depths of your soul. Once the chatter of the mind is shut off, the phenomenal silence brings to life the peace you so badly need in times of distrust and non-belief. You devote time every day to maintaining the positive by practicing affirmations. You have the faith to trust that the Source will always provide you with everything you need and you give thanks through prayer.

Teach your readers how to get started with meditation and encourage them along the way. So much is available that has been sent to receptive minds on Earth. It is for this purpose that the books have been written, along with many other wonderful resources. Once the commitment is made, the intention is clear, and the direction understood, your readers will find that opportunities to learn and grow will present themselves in the most profound ways.

Q. What else do you have to say on meditation?

A. Meditation has been practiced on the earth for thousands of years, mainly in Eastern cultures. It is the supreme connection to the higher self, or Godself. Through your own studies, you have learned that prayer is talking, while meditation is listening.

Now, there are four levels of consciousness:

- *Beta*, the frequency of being fully awake, walking around, going about everyday business.
- *Alpha*, which is slightly removed from everyday waking. This is very easy to achieve and the level in which meditation takes place. It is also the level hypnotherapists and doctors use for biofeedback, for this is a powerful state in respect to the mind-body connection. Although one is still awake and aware of everything going on, the subconscious "opens" and is able to respond to suggestions. This is why sometimes during "active" meditation you are able to see and feel things that you would not normally see. During a normal day, each one of you reaches the alpha level at least 40 times. Watching TV, daydreaming during a boring lecture, mental drifting while driving a car, and gardening are just a few examples. How many times has someone been talking and you hear them but your mind is far away and you don't have a clue what was said? And when driving, have you ever found yourself wondering what happened to the last ten miles? Or you don't remember taking an exit.
- *Theta*, sometimes called the dream-state, occurs when one is deeply asleep and dreaming takes place. Drug-induced patients slip into this condition from which it is very difficult to rouse them.
- *Delta* is the unconscious or comatose state. Many who are close to death reach this level, and it is here that they actually cross over to our world to be shown what awaits them on this side. When I was in the comatose state, I remember going in and out of my body quite a bit. I would stare at the "shell" in the bed and wonder why something more couldn't be done. I was also getting glimpses of the other world. Daniel and Noel assured me that it was okay to let go. My Mom was there extending her hand. I was with you while you wept. When you and my family spoke to me at the bedside, I heard every word, but I couldn't communicate back. It was as if I was paralyzed and had no control.

There are three types of meditation:

- *Active meditation* takes place when you have dropped into the alpha state and actually receive thoughts, ideas and images. Many writers, artists and musicians credit their work to these unknown sources. Most of this material comes from lofty spirits in the fourth spiritual level and is sent to receptive minds on Earth. Active meditation may involve communication with angels, spirit guides and deceased loved ones, such as our process of "automatic dictation."

- *Self-directed meditation* involves acute focus on a certain insight or idea in order to master it or change it. For example, if you are ill, you can use biofeedback and positive mind imagery to program the subconscious mind to accept the suggestion that you are indeed well. Or you might work on financial gain, peace, spiritual insight, guidance, health, life purpose, work situations, or overcoming certain obstacles. The great masters and gurus have all used this technique to shed negative aspects of their earthly existences.

- *Passive meditation* is the total relaxation of body and mind. (Remember, Noel taught you that there is a big difference between resting and relaxing!) You close out the chatter of the mind and go to a safe place, one that allows you to just *be*. The real you. Deep inside is a silence in which you are most closely connected. The silence is a void, deep and penetrating, that yields a sense of fullness, a richness. It is important to note that before retreating to the silence, you let go of all of the problems and stresses of the day. When the body and the mind are completely relaxed, the stillness will follow. Here, you will be given the answers and the spiritual empowerment vital to your soul's growth and development. Your understanding may not come right away, but hours, days or even weeks later, you will discover great changes taking place. One of the greatest benefits of meditation is a magnificent transcendence—a feeling of well-being that no drug could possibly give.

After you start daily meditation and truly commit to it, you will long to continue in order to stay balanced and centered. After a while, you will spend longer amounts of time in this silent retreat. However, tranquility alone should not be the only goal of passive meditation. First and foremost should be the gaining of wisdom to take action in your life. Quiet solitude is a temporary retreat from the outer world, but even-tually you must deal with it. And in this wondrous state, you will find the means to overcome and master your limitations.

One of the misconceptions about meditation is that you will some-how be transformed into someone else, a dropout maybe, sitting on a mountaintop. This will not happen. Reaching higher consciousness or spiritual awareness does not result in *external* changes. The transforma-tions are truly *internal* since you are remembering who you really are—spirit having a human experience, rather than a human having a spiritual experience.

Many people have a problem with actually committing to medita-tion. How many times have you heard, "I know I need to meditate but I can't relax. I'm too stressed." Meditation is, in fact, a therapy for reliev-ing stress and brings relaxation almost immediately. But you must *want* to do it.

You must want to start leading a better, more successful and fulfill-ing life. Your students come up with weak excuses, such as, "I know I need to start meditating but I don't have the time." It's not that they don't have the time, but that they don't feel that nurturing themselves is important enough! There seems to be time for making sure all of their material possessions are in working order, but when it comes to their bodies, their minds, their spiritual well-being, priorities become scrambled. The commitment to meditate every day is more important than how much time you actually spend doing it. Everyone manages to do at least *one* unproductive task a day, so why not spend this time on something that will make an enormous difference in how you perceive the world, the people in it and your own self? Stop the insanity in the mind and start dealing with life in a lighter mood. Begin the day whistling and humming instead of fighting with others. Be kinder, gentler and more loving. Be successful and happy. And most importantly, gain peace.

There are hundreds of successful meditation methods. Please advise your readers to investigate the different techniques to find one they are most comfortable with. Your world is full of books on the subject, classes to attend, and other helpful tools. Rather than sleep over here, we medi-tate, and I would like to introduce some of my favorites. I'm excited to contribute some of the teachings I've acquired in my own search for en-lightenment here. I'll try to keep it simple as some of your readers will be beginners. As they progress, they can explore more advanced techniques.

To prepare for any type of meditation:

- Equip a quiet room for meditation with candles and soft music. Flowers are always nice because of the sweet aroma they bring, although you may wish to burn incense. The time of day does not matter but should be a time when you will not be disturbed.
- Choose whichever meditation position is most comfortable. I suggest sitting or reclining as opposed to lying down to avoid falling asleep.
- Wear loose clothing and remove your shoes. Place your hands by your sides, palms up, with the thumb and first finger of each hand touching. This is so that the prana, or life energy, is balanced as it flows freely between levels of consciousness. Slowly close your eyes.
- Try to empty your mind of all hostility, stress and problems. Meditation is not the place to bring negativity! With eyes closed, imagine yourself sitting on the edge of the world, looking out at the universe and seeing the planets and stars in all their beauty. Now with one great toss, throw out all of the garbage; all the anxiety and tension that have built up; all the worries and concerns and hate. Just let it all go, sending it out into the cosmos with the intention that it be transformed into positive energy. You have no use for it any longer, and it is hindering your growth. Instead, tell the universe that you are seeking truth and peace. Ask that it be given to you during your meditation.
- Say a prayer for protection to ensure that nothing comes between you and the Source during the altering of consciousness. Do not be fearful of meditation, as it is very safe, but be aware that there are dark forces that would feel right at home invading your space and making it difficult to concentrate. Prayer also helps to keep the energy "grounded" to maintain proper re-entry into the beta state.

Meditate every day for about ten or fifteen minutes. Increase the time gradually as the days go by. The key here is consistency. Remember that the *commitment* is more important than how much time you spend doing it. And approach it playfully, without unrealistic expectations.

Meditation #1

With eyes closed, begin breathing in through the nose and back out through the mouth. Your aim is to concentrate only on the breath going in and out. Breathing sustains you, and you cannot survive without it for more than a few minutes. Some refer to this life energy as pranic energy or prana. Continue breathing in and out, in and out, letting the rhythm of this force bring you to a higher level, relax you and empty the mind. Relax and breathe, that's all. When thoughts come, just observe them and let them go. Don't try to analyze. Return to the breath. In and out, in and out.

Once you feel comfortable, begin repeating a word that represents total and blissful peace. Any word will do. It can be God, Love, Light or any other word that moves you into serenity. Repeat it with every breath in and every breath out. Let your being flow with the breath and the word. Become one with them, flowing, relaxing, breathing. White light is now surrounding you and is you. It signifies the love of the Divine. Allow this white light to become a part of the flow that now encompasses you. Stay here now, and enjoy the peace. And know that all is being given to you.

Meditation #2

This exercise emphasizes the beauty of stillness. It can also be used in preparation for the death process. With eyes closed, rest your elbows on a table or a pillow on your lap. Use your fingers to pinch the ears shut. Now listen. The sound you hear is your own tone, your own frequency, and the sound of your soul, connecting you with the universal energy of the Source. It is similar to what you might hear in a seashell— the sound of the ocean, or a waterfall. There are other similarities in the sound but you will know what I mean when you hear it.

Let this sound move through you until the flow is such that you become part of it and it part of you. The object is not to hear, but to *listen*. At some point, as you develop this exercise, you will experience a burst of light. This is the light of your soul. When you can see this light for one minute without interference, you have successfully reached an intense level of consciousness. Your vibrations are extremely powerful when raised to this level of awareness. You will begin to realize the significance of the "I AM" one-ness of the universe and its connecting Source. This sense of purity will bring you closer and closer to enlightenment. (At some point there will be no need to manually close the ears.) Use this meditation to clarify and gain peace.[3]

Q. How about prayer? Many people here are confused, so can you clarify?

A. Let me start by telling you what prayer is NOT. The act of praying should not be seen as you, the shopper, with your shopping list of things to ask for. The Source is not a vending machine. People can ask and ask, and then wonder why their "wishes" are not granted. Prayer is not a time for foolery. You cannot hide your intentions from your spirit, for it *is* you.

Who or what is the target of prayer? It is a request to the Universal Intelligence to intercede on your behalf. Even bringing in Reiki energy is a form of prayer. Prayer is very powerful, so powerful that even a kind or sympathetic "thought" concerning someone who is having problems is a prayer in itself! It is the letting go of *all that is not love* and replacing it with *all that is love*, for prayer is rooted in love. It is also perfectly acceptable to pray for yourself. Affirm that you have understanding and direction when you are confused. Affirm that you are filled with love and strength when tragedy hits. And above all, offer gratitude for the wisdom to help you to survive and move forward. Pray with trust to this glorious entity that cannot be seen with the physical eye, for that is the faith of which I have already spoken. You can pray with false gratitude, but the absence of sincerity will always rear its ugly head. The aim must always be for the highest good.

Again, prayer is a most powerful exercise and is the acceptance of both the Source as Light and love, of the Divine part of you. Pray with conviction, openness, belief and faith.

You can pray while walking, standing, sitting or however is comfortable for you to focus all of your devotion and attention on your prayer. Pray in gratitude as though what you have requested has already been given. It is always good to offer gratitude for all of your blessings, even when things are going well. Sadly, there are some who only pray when they have hit rock bottom.

Some see the Divine as the cause of their problems but, oftentimes, the situation they are in is caused by their own zealousness or something that could have been avoided. Please tell everyone that during these times, your guides, your own spirit, and even the Source, are with you and ready to assist.

Affirm that you have wisdom and guidance in your journey. The Source is an observer, not a problem-solver, for you all have free will and the ability to make choices. Trust that every prayer is heard but nothing can countermand your actions and free will.

People may say, "God should know everything I need, so why should I pray?" To them I say, "The act of praying surrenders you to open up, to enable you to tune into that light inside of yourself which *is* the Divine, and to accept what is given. For prayer is manifestation through thought, and the outcome is based on faith and belief.

What I'm about to say may sound like New Age psychobabble but it will have to be covered sooner or later. Let me first start by explaining the different levels of the mind. The conscious mind is the rational part with which you make all of your decisions. Its tools are reason and analysis. It is most closely tied to the physical body.

The unconscious mind is intuitive, sometimes referred to as the Infinite Intelligence, the soul, the Higher Self, the "God" part of you. Universal wisdom in its purest form is contained here. Every solution and answer your spirit seeks is hidden in its depths.

The subconscious mind is a *microcosm* of the unconscious and is closest to the spirit. It is where the unconscious is constantly "dumping" requested information during prayer and meditation and is the storehouse of memory. It also keeps your blood flowing, your kidneys working, your heart beating and all of the processes that don't require conscious direction. It does not reason or analyze, and will not dispute what you tell it, but simply takes the suggestion (cause) and delivers the result (effect). It accepts as true whatever the conscious mind believes to be true and is therefore highly open to suggestion.

Now, understanding from our earlier discussion that the Source is not a separate being from you or I, it follows that when you pray, you are actually connecting with the Universal Mind, Source, Intelligence, whatever—*of which you are a part!* The subconscious mind processes your prayer and the result depends upon your belief system, so your beliefs must consist only of faith and love. If fear and doubt are lurking in the shadows, what comes to pass will be based on that fear. This is why it's so important to *affirm* what you seek through prayer.

If you state, "I wish I had more money," your subconscious will take you literally and arrange for you to continue *wishing* you had more money! If instead, you affirm, "I have been blessed with financial gain," is affirmed with the faith that what you seek has already been given, then the subconscious will do everything in its power to draw to you all of the circumstances that signal abundance. Thoughts are extremely powerful and will manifest according to belief.

The Source answers in many ways: Through feelings, thoughts, events and people who appear at just the right time in your lives, and, of course, during meditation, when you are most profoundly connected.

"And whatever you ask in prayer, you will receive, if you have faith."[4]

"Therefore I tell you, whatever you ask in prayer, believe you will receive it, and you will."[5]

Q. Why is it that some do not receive the miracles they pray for?

A. This ties in with what I just said. First of all, the word "miracle" refers to something that is inexplicable by natural forces, so is attributed to a supernatural agent, for example, when a terminally ill child is completely cured of disease. A tiny acorn growing into a giant oak tree, the birth of a baby, your car stalling just as you were about to drive over a railroad crossing as a train approaches—these are all miracles. Sometimes even death is a miracle.

When someone prays to a higher power for a miracle, something will result from the request, but it may take an unexpected form. The outcome will reflect what is perfect for the soul, and that may differ greatly from what's requested. For example, a mother may be distraught over her young daughter being close to death following an accident. So, in the hospital chapel, she prays to God to please let her daughter live. This would be her miracle. The child dies soon after and the mother is angry with God for not saving her daughter's life. In her grief, she does not realize that the miracle was actually allowing this child to die because the little girl would have had severe brain damage and maybe other health problems. Suffering, anxiety and pain for her and her family were not part of her soul's plan.

So where is the miracle when a child *does* survive an accident but must live with various handicaps? The miracle is the love and devotion of family and friends, the specialness of this child who teaches everyone around her to live life to the fullest, taking nothing for granted. Her great sacrifice and strength will teach many valuable lessons. Do not focus on the tragedy, but on how you react to and confront it. It is in this experience that you will see the miracle.

So you see, miracles do occur. They occur every day, many of which you're not even aware happen, such as synchronistic events that lead you away from danger or harm. But they happen according to what is *needed*, not necessarily what is *wanted*.

Q. Would you please discuss the role of angels and spirit guides in our lives?

A. We here all wonder why this is such a hard concept for you all to understand, but I keep reminding myself that it was equally as difficult for me to penetrate the belief when I was there. Your angels and spirit guides touch your lives every day. They are your teachers and have only your soul's balance at heart. Your spirit guides have mastered certain lessons during previous earth lives and have chosen to assist you in this way.

Angels have not spent any time on the Earth plane but have been created and taught to serve mankind from here. The main difference between angels and spirit guides is that spirit guides have actually lived physical lives in the earth. They have attained such incredible wisdom that they choose this mission of hope to guide and direct from the other dimension. Many famous people of Earth have had the pleasure of spiritual visions and inspirations, such as Joan Of Arc, Mozart, Einstein, Edison, and, of course, Nikola Tesla, a child prodigy and electrical genius, whose visions and inspirations brought him much success and admiration, from everyone except his bitter rival, Edison, that is.

To be in an angel's presence is to be forever changed, as you were, Walda, when you met Noel. I remember thinking how calm and centered you seemed to be with your new assurance of the angelic/spiritual realms. Let me now dispel some misconceptions.

Angels do not have wings. It is actually the shimmering light around them and the flowing of their clothing that is deceptive. Their halos are actually the glow of the aura around their heads. And, no, they don't carry harps!

Spirit guides and angels do not ask that you be perfect. They do ask, however, that you strive for perfection in understanding the principle of love. Your guides are yours and no one else's, and are in perfect balance with your soul's journey. They never scold, but are loving and attentive, just as a good parent might be. They guide you gently with soft touches and subtle signs.

Spirit guides and angels are assigned to you at birth, depending on what you need to accomplish and master in your lifetime. For example, you were destined to write and Nora stood back until it was time. Now she is assisting you, with me. She "produces" the concept of what we will write and was especially helpful with Part One of this book because of its heavy emotional content. Noel is what we here call a master teacher, and is quite evolved spiritually.

I'm told that master teachers remain with a person through many lifetimes, and since they are androgynous, you may perceive them at different times as either male or female. Their faces may change from time to time, and this ability to take different forms denotes the status of master. After death, you will continue to have contact with one or two master guides or angels since there is still so much to learn and accomplish here.

Angels are Light Beings of the purest energy and vibrate at an extremely high rate, which is why they are rarely seen with physical eyes. They are unconcerned with having names but know that humans need names in order to communicate, so their purpose is paramount, they often give you a name that signifies their mission with you.

Although you have chosen many angels and spirit guides for your growth, your spirit may call in specialized beings to help with healing, meditation and other tasks. Your guides keep you on the course that you chose before birth—the supreme plan, if you will—so do not expect an angel or guide to tell you the future, for they cannot override your free will by interfering with your decisions and choices. However, they will gently nudge you in the right direction, but you must use your inner guidance to listen to them, to recognize the clues and signs, and to be ever watchful of the synchronicities and miracles that abound in everyday life.

I will not go into all the classifications of angels since many great books already describe the hierarchies and classes. Suffice to say that your spirit guides and angels are *always* with you, and that *no one is ever alone.*

Tell your readers that when they are feeling down, lonely, depressed, and thinking that no one hears them or cares, they are wrong. If you would learn to connect with Spirit, you would not feel so hopeless and lost as many often do. Meditation will bring you closer to the spiritual and angelic realms, and hopefully the peace you seek. You need only open yourself to experience the love and protection that Spirit represents. Belief and trust are the key words here, for it is through Spirit that the Divine Voice is heard.

Be quiet and *listen*.

Q. Synchronicity has become a popular topic lately. Can you shed some light on it?

A. You are referring to "meaningful coincidence," a term coined by Carl Jung. It is a synchronization of inner and outer events without the usual cause and effect of *physicality*. When it happens, it is meaningful and leaves no doubt that something profound is going on. For example, you may be thinking of an old friend and shortly after "accidentally" meet him or her on the street.

The universe is a vast network of free-flowing thoughts, ideas and events, some of which are actually guiding forces in your lives. Synchronicity is perceived when your angels, guides and deceased loved ones intervene in moving you along your life plan. This is spiritual guidance in its highest form, with signs and clues that reveal your soul's goals for this lifetime.

Sometimes it's necessary to look beyond the analytical, left-brain methods for direction. At a crossroad, many people tend to see only what is logical to the ego as it tries to convince them to "be sensible." And in doing so, you may miss important signs, causing you to repeat the same lessons over and over. Some of you will remain left-brained for your entire lifetime while others, after being "bonked" over the head several times, will finally understand how the right brain can assist you in moving joyfully forward in your progress.

There are valuable ways to receive direction and guidance, and you need only to recognize these subtle hints sent from spirit. Synchronicity is not controlled by outer events; it is how your inner self sends signals to your outer self. Awareness of these will allow you to spot synchronistic information so that you can use it to advance your growth.

Signs can come in the form of dreams, meditation and intuitive hunches. It can also show itself as the smallest clue that appears repeatedly, such as glancing at your digital clock whenever it shows 11:11. Synchronicity can fulfill the spirit in many ways. It can teach faith, love, forgiveness and compassion. It can also lead people to their destinies in terms of career, relationships, and life purpose. In addition, it can direct the troubled toward good fortune and blessings.

For example, two people here had planned before birth to complete a lesson or task together, so their angel guides did everything possible to bring them together After being introduced, each felt a deep, spiritual connection to the other. They kept running into each other in remote parts of the globe. Hints and clues were sent but neither was "listening." Finally, in a last ditch effort to unite them, their guides devised a plan. The woman had a dream in which she was shown a phone number, and nothing else. Immediately on waking, she wrote the number down and called out of sheer curiosity. To her utter amazement, she discovered that it was the very same man she had already met on several occasions, and they both agreed that they should become better acquainted. They were married soon after, had five successful children and completed many life lessons together.

Again, this assistance is the free-flow of the universe, sent to you by Spirit. Please stress to your readers the importance of learning to detect this guidance when it is given, and most importantly, to act upon it.

Q. I've been struggling with the concept of God for a long time, and through intense prayer and meditation, I finally realize that God is the ultimate All That Is, and that this Divine Creator is not separate from me. What's your perspective?

A. To start off, God is called by many different names depending on what your beliefs are. However, this is of no concern, because there is only one Source and it matters not what you call it. It is without gender, or I should I say that it's both male and female.

It's impossible to describe this Supreme Intelligence to you who live in the material plane because many of you are looking for a simple explanation in physical terms, and quite frankly, there isn't one. But, without getting deep into metaphysical theory, I'll do my best.

When I died, I believed in an angry, judgmental male God, and that's what I was afraid of encountering. When I was first in God's presence, I felt unworthy and afraid because I didn't want to experience His angry judgment. I was pleasantly surprised to discover that I was just as worthy as anyone else and also that the Source was not angry with me at all. On the contrary, I felt overwhelming waves of unconditional love and peace in that presence and became part of this Universal Source. I learned then that God's will was actually *my* will and that I needed to stop viewing the Source as being *outside* of myself.

The Divine has no beginning and no end—it just is; all knowing, all being and "All That Is." Made up of brilliant light and love energy, its wisdom is incomprehensible even to those of us who've been here a while. We just know that to be in this presence is to blend with its magnificence and feel its love through an elation that has no human words to describe it. Through this energy, we are all connected as one. Earlier, I used the analogy of us being drops of water that make up the river. One drop unto itself may not be as all-powerful as the entire river, but it is nevertheless "river stuff."

Many people lose faith because they say God is unseen. On the contrary, I now know that the Supreme is in everything everywhere, and I mean *everything everywhere*—every rock, tree, bird, and grain of sand. There is Divine Intelligence in everything. What makes a tiny acorn grow into a giant oak tree? What creates the tide? And what causes a lump of coal to become a diamond? This Universal Intelligence is ever flowing through this expansive cosmos. And this is God manifested!

This Source is powerful only according to what our soul chooses to do. It cannot interfere with our free will but does send comfort and strength through our faith. It responds to every prayer, although the outcome may not be what you were looking for. This Creative Force does not give us what we want, but what we *need* for the easiest journey possible. It is up to us to accept the gift, as the Creator strives to make us co-creators with it. Taking this one step further, we are all gods, since it is through this Creative Intelligence that we are able to manifest whatever we need to live joyfully.

Faith is the key here, but the trick lies in knowing the difference between faith through love and faith through fear. Faith through fear obviously doesn't work, and we learn this the hard way. You may say, "I have faith but my problems are still here." This is because you think that you are trusting God, but doubt and fear still occupy your thoughts.

Faith through love on the other hand is an absolute, undeniable belief in the Source and its unconditional love. It is both an intensely powerful, unstoppable force, yet very delicate. Faith is not a wish or a request, as in "Dear God, make my problems go away," or "Heal my sick body." Faith is an unquestionable trust in the Source and its ability to manifest in your life. This is trust in its purest form, and through this, the obstacles in your life will suddenly become surmountable. As you work at mastering the lessons needed for your soul development, the Source is there when you are ready to surrender the outcome. And your journey will always be joyful.

Surrender to the fact that *you will see it when you believe it* and not the other way around. For when you truly believe, know and trust in the Universal Source, without needing constant proof of its existence, you will finally begin to recognize the many miracles in your life.

Pray with *thanksgiving* for your many blessings. If you think you have nothing to be thankful for, search deep down in your soul until you find something. The Source will rejoice in your commitment to love and your detachment from fear. And you will *never* walk alone.

Q. What is your perspective on love and forgiveness?

A. This is one of my personal favorites because I was fortunate enough, while on Earth, to experience the most passionate love with you, my woman.

If you were to ask me what the secret to the universe was, I would answer, "Love." Only love is real. Love is an all-powerful energy, the ultimate creating force, and the most compelling emotion in the universe. It originates *in* all of us and *for* all of us from the Source itself. This means that when you love someone, it's not *that* person's love you feel, but the love inside of *yourself*. So when you give love, you are actually the receiver. The other person merely serves as a catalyst to set the wheels in motion. The obvious corollary is that if you do not love yourself, you cannot love another or feel another's love for you, hence the expression, "You must love yourself first."

Self-esteem, self-confidence, and self-love are critical, for how else could you recognize loving another? If you are dissatisfied with your body or your mind, or beat yourself up for past mistakes, you block the flow of the Source's love for you and become stagnant.

So, if you're treated poorly in a relationship, low self-esteem leads you to believe that your treatment is justified because who could ever love you, or who would want to receive your love? So, you see, really loving and respecting yourself are paramount. And then, knowing the intense sensation of love, you will want to send it out to as many people as you can.

You cannot really know love until you have experienced (either in this life or another) the fierce inequities of hatred. This will teach you the pain of being the target of someone's cruelty. Then, knowing the pain it causes, you are less likely to want to hurt someone else.

More and more young people grow up in dysfunctional families and do not have the experience of love in their lives. Mistaking infatuation for love, they hop from one troublesome relationship to the next. Confused, they may end up in a life of crime, unwanted pregnancy, drug abuse and hatred toward their fellow man. They blame their parents, their peers, and anyone else they can think of for their situation, but this is ego talking, for ego loves pain.

Forgiveness of self and of others will defuse the ego's arguments and bring "victims" to a state of acceptance and clarity that will enable them to stop dwelling on the fear and hatred in their lives, and instead focus on how much love and peace they can give to others.

Forgiveness does not mean "forget-ness." It means accepting where you are, moving on, and asking, "What have I learned from this?" But most important, it allows you to send love out to heal those who have caused you harm. Forgiving those people is a most courageous act but is the only way to true peace.

Love encompasses so much. Please tell your readers that self-love is the single most important area of spiritual work and, through a commitment to meditation and prayer, you can change this for the better.

Love is so intensely powerful that just the nurturing a baby gets from its parents can begin to weave the peaceful life he will lead. Love is almost as important as oxygen to human beings. A few kind words here, or a gentle touch there, are more precious than you can imagine. Try sending love to someone who has hurt you and feel the peace it brings, not only to yourself but to the other person, as well. Here in our world, we are fortunate in having an overabundance of love from which to draw, but we have earned this.

Unconditional love may be harder for readers to grasp. Unconditional means loving someone no matter what. A child misbehaves but still you love him. Of course, you teach him right from wrong so that he understands, but you do it with kindness. Your spouse is unfaithful but still you love him or her because you married for better or for worse and will persevere to save the marriage. But even after separation or divorce, your love for him or her should not dissolve because, if nothing else, he or she has been one of your greatest teachers, and the behavior is exactly according to the pre-life agreement the two of you drew up.

AIDS patients challenge you to love without conditions. Ostracized because of their lifestyle, and lying in a hospice waiting to die, their families are nowhere to be found. Would those family members turn their backs if their relative were dying of cancer instead?

Please remember that everyone incarnates with a purpose, and makes choices in alignment with that plan. We are all headed in the same direction of growth and evolution, but we each take our own particular route, so if you choose to fly, and others choose to walk, their journey is not less significant than yours, and they should not be looked upon with impatience. Indeed, honor them, for these are the ones who are truly taking the time to learn as well as to teach.

How a person looks—the outer shell of the body—is not what matters. That's just an *illusion*. I repeat, *the body is an illusion!* If you didn't have your five senses, how would you be able to relate to anyone? Here, we interact at a profound level of sensing and knowing through telepathy, and with our entire being—spirit and soul—for that is who you *really* are. You all have the ability to tap into a person's real self and see that he or she is exactly like you, made of the same "God-stuff." It's up to you to recognize it and "water" it with compassion. For the way to love is to *be* love. Forget judgment. You cannot know enough about other people's life plans to judge them or the challenges they took on for this lifetime. And it doesn't serve you to do this. *Your only job is to love by being love.*

Since *being* love is your mission of service, you don't have to *do* anything.

Just *be*. Plain and simple.

Q. Tom, why did you choose a public occasion to have your heart attack? And how closely involved was your spirit in planning the precise details?

A. Actually, Walda, you and I both agreed on it for several reasons. I could have passed out of this life on several occasions—maybe in my sleep or driving the van back from New York the previous day. But together we decided on this rather large summer gathering of almost one hundred people mainly because of the comfort and support we knew you would need from our friends and family. At the spirit level, you were unsure of how prepared your personality would be for this tragic moment and wanted the extra insurance of having our loved ones standing by.

Another reason was because of the effect it would have on the many onlookers. It was a wake-up call for some who took life for granted. And it gave some the opportunity to lend a hand during your time of suffering. The "Divine Computer" and karmic ties are really amazing, aren't they? The last reason was because I loved all of our friends and family so much and knew I would miss them terribly. I wanted the last things I experienced to be joyful and filled with a festive atmosphere. And you know how much I enjoyed an *audience* while on the earth.

As far as my spirit planning this so precisely, people must understand how incredibly involved their spirit is with their moment-by-moment human life. It is so intimately involved that every step you take is orchestrated through your spirit. Remember, your spirit is constantly striving to *remember* by experiencing and *being*. It unconsciously knows all of the soul's choices and works with conviction to carry out the plan. It welcomes the nudges from your guides and the Higher Self but is also aware that free will is very strong.

Unconsciously, my spirit had been planning my death circumstances for quite a while. Except for some minor details, it was carried out in direct alignment with both our souls' plans. To ensure the precise outcome, I was "nudged" to put extra stress on my heart and lungs by lifting the heavy boxes the day before, overdoing it at the gym that morning, and being as active as possible at the party. I wanted to make sure it happened where, when and how it had been so carefully planned.

While I was planning my departure, I kept thinking of how much I wanted to be able to say goodbye to you and to share some closure time together. That was why Daniel kept sending me signs several weeks before to make me go to the doctor. But this was not part of the plan you and I had chosen and I wanted to remain steadfast to our agreement.

Does the plan always work so flawlessly? Unfortunately, no, because people do not always "listen" and follow their intuition. The spirit can only do so much, which is why it's important for you to connect with your Higher Self and follow the "path" it has chosen. Your spirit is amazingly powerful, but it can carry out the highest and best intents and purposes of your soul's plan only if you will allow it to do so and follow its guidance. And let me emphasize once more, *there is never a time when your spirit is not involved in what you're doing. Never.*

Q. Tom, why did you try so hard to reach me after your death? And how did you feel about my initial resistance?

A. After my funeral was over and things had calmed down, I began talking to you as I had done during my transition into spirit. I was so happy knowing that you were "receiving." But Daniel told me that, even though our intense love for each other had allowed us to overcome the biggest hurdle, it would be up to you to choose to accept the process. And you kept resisting, even though I "nudged" you to resume meditation, which you'd abandoned after my death. In fact, you resisted even more, because of your fear of not knowing how to handle this. And you were also afraid that you might be having a breakdown. All that fear really blocked you, and Daniel and I actually thought you may not choose to take part.

Daniel told me that if you decided against the communication, then we must honor your choice. Of course, back then, I was less aware than I am now and still carried some of my earthly emotions, so the chance that you may not choose to participate caused me a great deal of frustration, to the point that my progression here may have been halted. However, using some synchronistic events, Daniel and some of the others helped me introduce you to Patricia Mischell. Had it not been for her, your trust in the Source, and your guidance from Noel, you probably would have chosen to avoid of all of this. I still feel your 'occasional resistance but at least I know now that I finally have your attention.

The reason I tried so hard to contact you brings us to the crucial topic of pre-life agreements. Now, you and I have shared thousands of incarnations and are part of an ancient "old soul" energy. The term "old soul" has nothing to with age, because all souls were "created" at exactly the same moment. It has to do with the evolution of a soul's *wisdom*. I said earlier that the soul makes choices before each incarnation and our souls opted to be together once more. (When you come here, you will meet all of your previous incarnations. They are all here, as are mine.)

When I died, I was initially angry and thought that there was no justice. I did not want to be "here" knowing you were "there." We had so much planned together, and it didn't seem fair for me to die so young. And my love for you was a blazing inferno of ecstasy and I couldn't imagine not being able to hold you and be with you. But because of your deep love for me, and the prayers you and our loved ones sent, I quickly moved into acceptance. Once I did, I was shown our destinies and the pre-life agreements we had made. Suddenly it all made sense and I understood why things happened the way they did. As I became more familiar with my surroundings and my new consciousness, I was able to shed my earthly concepts of "loss" and "victim," and become one with the Divine Intelligence.

As part of our life plans, we had vowed to assist mankind in a most profound way. The timing was perfect, as this is a period of great awareness on Earth—a time when consciousness is being researched and people are discovering their spirituality. Events turned out exactly the way we had planned—a fairly normal existence and then we would lose it all— which we did. This was to lead to your spiritual awakening, which would fully prepare you to take my death and transform it into a means to help others. Death is the ultimate event in life, and mankind must learn to understand death in order to realize the spiritual aspect of who they really are!

Unfortunately, in some people, the truth is buried so deeply that their journeys are often difficult and filled with needless suffering. I will say it again. *It doesn't have to be that way!* You can learn without the pain and sadness. And often, the pain and sadness actually get in the way of mastering the lessons, so you undergo incarnation after incarnation of the same scenarios. So you, my woman, will educate the weary and the grieving. You will bring light into a dark world. You will bring peace to an angry existence. And you will bring love to all of the lives you touch.

Another pre-life agreement we shared was to raise our son, a very special soul who has traveled with us before. His energy is not as evolved as ours, but he came to us as both a blessing and a responsibility. He required two parents who would give him the structure and life tools he would need to become a respected historian and theologian. These included strict morals, unwavering guidance, a middle-class upbringing and an incredible amount of unconditional love. He, too, is on his own path, and chose us to be his guardians on earth. Since his spiritual beliefs are very different from yours, you will both teach each other. And you will assist him in understanding the meaning of unconditional love.

Q. I have no doubt that the "communication" from you was real, but I'm curious about how you actually performed the events I described in Part One.

A. This is a very significant topic and one that deserves a place in this book. But first, let me point out that I am still learning how to translate from spirit to human, and speak from the *unlimited* dimension of spirit into the *limited* dimension of the physical.

As we discussed earlier, as spirit, we are an extremely sensitive energy. The mind holds the everlasting consciousness energy, which survives death and moves us to a higher consciousness and dimension. *It is pure, creative, thought energy.* The longer we are in this world of Love and Light, the stronger our energy becomes. *Everything* in the physical world is composed of vibrating energy, so we can "activate" things there from here because, to us, there really is no "here" and "there," but just different frequencies.

The minute I was taken down with my heart attack, I found that I could still make an impact on you. As soon as I left my body at the party, I knew what had happened. I was incredibly agitated, and you were the first person I thought of. Poof! I was immediately with you. I wanted you to know I was trying to re-enter my body even as our friends tried to resuscitate me so that we could continue our wonderful life together.

Although my body was unconscious and unresponsive, my spirit energy was embracing you and you were very aware of this. Daniel told me, "This connection was easy for the two of you because your love bond is so intense that it allowed you, through materialization, to create a physical sensation in Walda." It was more than a sensing for you, and it was so powerful that you had no choice but to acknowledge it. That's the tingling or vibrating that you now know so well.

As I drifted in and out of my body, I begged Daniel to let me live. He was gentle with me and allowed me to "stay" a little longer as I began the journey into my new existence. He told me to concentrate really hard and to imagine you and I as a single entity. I felt electrified as my thoughts of the love that we shared intensified until, suddenly, I felt a "pop" and we blended consciousness. Then you could feel my apprehension, my thoughts, and my love for you. I know now that this is a very powerful form of telepathy, yet back then, I thought that death meant we would be separated. In our blend, you shared my thoughts of my impending death and knew that I was leaving. I told you I would try to stay as long as I could, but you, dear soul mate of mine, courageously let me go and watched as I walked peacefully into the Light. We both somehow knew, on an unconscious level, that this was part of our pre-life agreement.

Since that day, we have never been apart. You accepted this new awareness with conviction, and, although there are still times when you cry out for me to come back physically, you are becoming more and more aware that a physical body isn't necessary for communication between our worlds.

I started to experiment with my newfound capabilities, and soon realized that the energy of my thoughts was actually the energy of creation! Not only could I connect with you, I could also make things happen to get your attention. I was shown how to "play" with electricity. This is what all novices like myself learn to perfect first. Because I am now such sensitive, high-frequency energy, activating electrical devices comes easily. By concentrating, I can direct the magnetic attributes of my energy to interact with electrical current. On Christmas Eve, 1996, I wanted so much to let everyone at our holiday gathering know for sure that I was there. I had planned to turn the power off for only a few minutes, and in our house *only*. However, my excitement caused misdirection in my focus and I blew out the power for the entire neighborhood! Although it was an innocent mistake, I knew I still had much to learn in my new existence.

Of course, the television is the easiest to control. It's as though I imagine myself *being* the television and controlling it from within. I loved to watch your expression as it changed channels and turned on and off. I always chose a sporting event to tell you that it was I, but as much as you wanted to believe that, you insisted that either the remote control or the television itself was at fault. And weren't you surprised when the new set arrived and nothing changed? Ironically, the new set was easier to work with!

The best part is the connection we now share. Our most intense communication has come through our meditations. At first, I had to lower my vibrations quite a bit because of your inexperience in raising yours. This was not easy for me, since after being in an unrestricted, limitless dimension, I had become used to the "lightness" of my being. Picture yourself weighted down with thirty or forty bricks tied around your body—it felt as if I had my physical body back again. Fortunately, you were soon able to raise your consciousness to a level that was comfortable for me. But I could feel your love pumping into me during these sessions and that's what kept me afloat. I knew you were trying hard and that it was necessary for us work together.

Patricia taught you well when she explained how to meditate through the heart chakra,[6] for this is what eventually raised your frequency and allowed us to reach a comfortable level of unity. Although you visited me quite often during your sleep, you couldn't remember these visits, so to be able to connect through meditation was a divine gift.

Thanks to our new "unity consciousness," we don't have to be meditating together for me to send you messages. I just have to get your attention and off we go. And vice versa. Whenever you have something to say, I'm with you in an instant. We're both still learning about translation, though, and sometimes I can't seem to convey my meaning in "earth" words so I resort to imagery, as with the time you were searching for my wedding ring. When you finally gave up and asked me to help, either you weren't picking up what I was saying or I wasn't transmitting clearly. That's when I "appeared" to you in the shirt I was wearing the day I took the ring off. You "saw" me pull the ring out of the pocket and you instantly knew where the ring was. To be able to show myself to you this way is, again, only a matter of pure thought and focus. Your mind's eye was strong and "open" due to the intense exercises you had been practicing, so it was easy for me to direct your attention. As I went through the motions of showing you, I also sent you the *idea*. I was thrilled at the connection and amazed at my command of the process.

When you almost threw out our bureau with $1,000 taped to the inside, you thought it was empty, but I knew differently. So I directed all my energy and focused on getting your attention. You heard me tell you, "Check again," and you watched as I showed you an envelope. Again, I had to use imagery to relate the information.

Daniel tells me that my emotional level has a lot to do with the clarity of my expression. If I'm overly excited, (which was my nature on Earth), my energy "scatters" and the connection is dissipated. Of course, the longer I'm here, the better I get and the more concentrated my energy becomes.

Q. Would you explain, Tom, how our guides brought you and I together?

A. Let me start out by saying that the following was revealed to me both during and directly after my life review. Learning the universal truths about Spirit guidance has been one of the most intense experiences I've had here in my new world.

Our first meeting was impeccably planned and carried out by the Divine through our guides. As you know, our purpose for coming into these particular incarnations was to do some very special work together, along with some leftover karmic balancing. There needed to be a burning, passionate love between us in order to make this work, for it would be through our intense love that this otherworldly connection would be made.

We met one very special night in 1966. Our lives up to this point had been in preparation for this event. You, Walda, had a very loving, compassionate heart and always rooted for the underdog. I was an underdog. I'd had a very tough childhood and no real direction in life. By the time we met, I was well on my way to being what some might call a juvenile delinquent. You were not materially rich but certainly much better off than I was, and I was the last person your parents had in mind for boyfriend-of-the month. But, it being the sixties, everyone mingled with everyone. No one traveled in cliques. Thank goodness for that, or we may have never met! (Another part of the plan!)

Our guides arranged this all with the most divine synchronicity. If you remember, you were at a sleepover at a girlfriend's house with about twenty other girls. Your guides made sure that you were there, despite some opposition from your strict father. You and your mother "softened" him up and off you went. The party was outside in the woods behind your friend's house. At age fourteen, you were in the midst of some innocent fun—popcorn, soda and a few cigarettes—but what's an all-girl party without some boys to crash it?

My best friend, Gary, and I had heard about it and decided to drop by to try and "score." My guides made sure that I was in the right place at the right time—I had run out of cigarettes and overheard someone in the store talking about this all-night party. By the time I arrived, it was in full swing and some people had begun to pair off, including you and your boyfriend at the time.

I'll never forget laying eyes on you for the first time. We looked deep into each other's souls and instantly fell madly in love. There was one difference between us— I couldn't admit that I had fallen head over heels for someone I didn't know. To my thinking, that just didn't happen. But you heard the whisperings of your spirit and began an outrageous flirting binge that lasted the entire night. Your boyfriend had already left the party early because of another commitment. Our guides as well as his, too, had carefully arranged this. We bonded incredibly and talked and laughed until the sun came up. There was something about you that I couldn't seem to shake. What was it? What was this overwhelming feeling? But you definitely weren't my type. I only dated the "in" girls. Fast and easy. My manhood and pride was on the line here and I had to make a choice. Investigate this further or let it go? I let it go.

When the gathering finally dispersed, it was like saying goodbye to an old friend. And for three years after that, you were never far from my mind, but despite your flirting and "chasing" me and my spirit and guides pushing me, I rebelled against the urge to ask you out. Your friends kept telling you I wasn't a good influence but you remained determined that we were life partners. Our guides were constantly nudging us in the form of dreams and the way you kept showing up in front of me. We always seemed to be in the same place at the same time, something I put down to coincidence, but the extent and complexity of the spirit guidance required to make this happen is beyond your limited senses to comprehend.

Finally, three years later, we officially became a couple. And I never looked back. We became one almost instantly and enjoyed 27 incredible years together. You were, and still are, more a part of me than you can know. And the passion still burns.

Q. How were our spirits guiding us when we both lost our jobs?

A. This was a pivotal point in our journeys. We had been so wrapped up in the material world that our spiritual base was at an all-time low. When we stood together at this crossroad in our lives, you began preparing for what was to come and needed to choose a path. You began seeking your truth from within and quickly started moving forward into the light. My path was different. I chose to stay connected to my possessions and struggled with how I would ever gain back what I had lost. I realized after my transition, that I had let my material worth control me and push aside my spiritual needs.

The experience was more for your benefit than for mine. We knew you would need quite a bit of direction and guidance to not only survive the tragedy of losing your life partner, but to turn it into something positive for others to learn from. The work that you and I would be doing would be intense and you needed to be on the highest and best path to carry it out.

Q. Tom, are there any instances you know of when I was guided before your death?

A. My wonderful wife, there is so much I could tell you about all the times when you have been divinely led but there are a couple that are most significant.

You were vacationing with your family, about six years old, and one morning, you sat alone on the dock waiting for your father to launch his motorboat in the lake. Suddenly, you heard a kitten meowing as though it was in pain. Where was it coming from? You followed the noise down to the other end of the long, wooden dock, and thinking that it might be trapped beneath the dock, you tried to look under it, but it was too dark, so you decided to go find a flashlight.

As you walked back to the trailer, you heard a loud crash, like thunder. A runaway speedboat had smashed into the dock, causing it to buckle and break exactly where you had been sitting. You would never have seen it coming because your back was turned to the lake. Had you not gotten up when you did, you would have been seriously injured. You were so upset about not being able to solve the mystery of the injured kitten that it never even occurred to you that you had just been guided to avoid a tragedy. Oh, and there never really was a kitten.

Another event took place in 1975. It was a Monday night, your regular night for running errands to the market, the cleaners, the bank, and then to downtown Lynn to a department store. You were such a creature of habit; nothing ever got in the way of your weekly routine, but this night something did. Your car wouldn't start so you got a jump-start from your uncle's truck. About a mile down the road, you got a flat tire, and again, your uncle came to the rescue. It was raining hard, and as you continued on, your windshield wipers stopped working. You finally decided that your errands were not worth the risk of an accident, so you turned around and cautiously drove home.

When you got home, I remember how irritated you were about your change of plans, but what you didn't know was that at the precise moment you would have been downtown, a gang fight erupted into a full blown riot. Several cars innocently passing through the area were caught in the crossfire and demolished. You would have been in one of those cars.

Had you ignored the "guidance," you would not have died, for it was not your time, but you may have been injured severely, which would have altered your life plan and impacted your direction. This was not your path at this time. If it had been, no such warnings would have been issued. In fact, you would have been guided into the thick of the fighting, with your guides providing necessary comfort and support as they worked for your highest and best interests for that growth experience.

Q. How and why did I choose my parents, what did I look for in them, and did they "deliver"?

A. Walda, you actually chose your parents not only for your soul's balance, or karma, but for theirs as well. The most significant part of this balance came at the end of their earth lives. The loving energy you gave to them during their months of illness and as they lay dying was monumental to their peaceful transitions. They were both so frightened and welcomed your loving touch and gentle words. You taught them so much in those last few months and made sure they were well taken care of. They both knew that they were loved and cherished.

In your father's case, he awakened you to the real meaning of forgiveness, as there had been quite a bit of anger in your heart for many years. And forgiveness is fuel for the soul's journey. As you watched your mother struggle to hold onto life, you learned about courage and strength. And these are the true lessons of the heart.

Did they deliver? Yes, I believe they did.

Q. What about mass death? Why do hundreds of people decide to die together in these tragedies? And how are "mass arrivals" handled on the other side?

A. This may sound cold, but tragedies are an element of human existence. We cannot "judge" them or blame the universe. No one on your side can know what the circumstances are behind the obvious misfortune of others. All you can do is pray for the victims and help in any way you can.

Plane crashes, monsoons, earthquakes, train wrecks and other disasters cause hundreds and thousands of simultaneous deaths. Someone on this side who attends one of the study groups tells of her experience in the Jonestown tragedy in Guyana some years ago. She chose this death to make the world aware of cults, and to allow her family to understand forgiveness, for she died with many unresolved issues between her and them. When she was instructed to drink the poison, she did so out of misguided love for the man she thought was God on earth, the Reverend Jim Jones. This mass sacrificial suicide opened the world's eyes and helped to balance the karma of the many who were affected by it.

As for mass arrivals, I must point out that in my world, there is no physical space as you would know it on Earth, so the question of how much "room" is available for the huge number of spirits involved is meaningless. At one point, while I volunteered in one of the many "hospital" centers here for the newly deceased, a large earthquake killed several thousand people. I was amazed at the organization and ease with which the situation was handled. Countless numbers of volunteer helpers poured in to assist the healing angel guides administering to the new arrivals who were so traumatized that they were in a complete state of shock. Watching them work was both fascinating and enlightening.

Many arrivals were unaware of what had happened and just wanted to return home to their loved ones. They were provided with food, clothing and shelter, for this is what they asked for. The babies and children were tended to by deceased relatives and, oddly enough, had the most peaceful transitions of all. Nurseries and playgrounds were quickly set up, complete with picnic tables and toys to keep all the children happy and busy.

I attended to the arrivals who knew what had happened and just needed to rest for a while before entering the next stage. As I worked with them, I remembered how wonderful it was to wake up and see a loving presence sitting next to me. These people would ask me where they were, and I would tell them softly that they had come home. My task was to ease the trauma of the abrupt change that accompanies sudden death. Sometime soon after, when they felt the time was right, their designated guides would escort them through the life review.

Another limitation we are free of here is that of time. When large numbers of people arrive "at the same time" from your perspective, from ours, time is infinitely expandable, so no one "waits in line to be seen" as in a hospital emergency room.

One of the most amazing things I saw in this work was how those on your side helped or hindered the victims in making it past the "boundary." Even though deceased loved ones and guides on this side were patiently urging them on, many arrivals were reluctant to come into the Light. Having undergone intense, traumatic death, many new arrivals react less to the presence of spirit and more to their fellow earth-based relatives. As a result, new arrivals are more willing to listen to those still on your side. So I urge those compassionate earth helpers among you to help guide your deceased loved ones across the bridge with a few gentle words.

To those left behind following a mass tragedy, I assure you that we are taking good care of your loved ones. They are assisted every step of the way and no one is ever alone.

Q. How is a "mass death" event put together?

A. Again, this may sound cold, but tragedies and disasters are an element of human existence. Try not to judge, analyze or blame the universe. Natural disasters such as earthquakes, floods and volcanoes happen because of intrinsic changes in the earth. Plane crashes, mass suicides and bombings are caused by man, although sometimes not intentionally.

Souls choose to be involved in these types of situations for the same reasons anyone else would have for choosing their life experiences. What needs to be accomplished? Who will be impacted? What will my loved ones learn from it? What will this do to help me gain what I need for my own soul's growth? Will this mass tragedy bring about world compassion? Will the people who come out to help learn humility and strength?

Some people choose to become involved not because they opted to before they came into this life, but because they did not "listen" to the guidance and higher wisdom from within to move away from the impending situation. So there are two types of guidance—one that attempts to move you *toward* an experience and another that seeks to move you *away* from it.

This is where the Divine "computer" comes into play. (Remember, the computer was created here long before the idea was sent to receptive minds in the earth.) I understand that the incredible complexity of this system is beyond human comprehension, but to us, it makes perfect sense. The experiences and lessons you wish to master are all recorded in your life plan. If being part of a disaster or mass death situation will satisfy the needs of your soul's balance, you will be guided toward an event of this type. If it is the designated time for your spirit to return home, you will be one of the fatalities. If you have chosen to learn or experience poverty, you will become one of the thousands of victims made homeless. And if you have chosen to experience illness or impairment so that, through you, your family can learn compassion, you will end up as one of the many injured. It is important to accept that you can't know what the circumstances are behind the obvious misfortune of others. All you can do is pray for the victims and help in any way you can.

What of the handful of survivors who emerge unscathed from a plane crash or an earthquake? They may have been guided into this event as a serious "wake-up call" in order to redirect their energy and focus on their life's lessons, plans and chosen missions.

So how do people know how to place themselves within the events needed for soul growth? Who works with these thousands of potential participants in helping them decide whether or not to take part? Very simply, Spirit does. The Source works through many forms, including deceased loved ones, angels and guides. The spirits of potential victims are "informed" that something is about to happen that "fits their plan." Don't forget that when you are in the sleep-state, tremendous communication takes place between the various levels of the psyche that makes up you. Unfortunately, you usually have no conscious memory of these conversations, but unconsciously, you carry around this universal knowledge and begin to prepare for what is about to happen, such as taking care of "unfinished business" and making amends with enemies.

Divine guidance takes place gently and precisely. Synchronicity is so delicate, yet so complex. I cannot emphasize enough just how closely the spirit is involved in your day-to-day life. Synchronistic events and intuition play a part in whether or not you decide to go into a public building that is about to be bombed or whether you car breaks down on the way to the airport.

Again, there are two types of guidance, one that steers you *away* from an event and another that directs you *toward* it. These seemingly free-flowing circumstances create an opportunity for you to experience, learn and remember whatever is necessary for your soul's development. And every moment of every day, you are being led and directed

Q. How can we help someone to have a peaceful transition?

A. Basically by being there fully and loving them unconditionally. When people are dying, they know it from somewhere deep in their soul, whether or not they have been consciously told. And they also know from the sudden change in attitude of those around them, the inaudible whispers and the extent of their care.

Typically, when a person has been labeled "terminal," the loved ones begin the grieving process, but please also spare a thought to the feelings of those who are dying. Often, their feelings are not recognized or acknowledged. No one thinks of them as grieving, but they do grieve, sometimes quite intensely. It is therefore critical that you share with them the most intimate details of the journey to come. It is indeed possible to take this journey together, sharing the joy and the pain.

Bring closure to the relationship by forgiveness and detachment from guilt. Instead of putting emphasis on the upcoming loss and sadness, enrich the remainder of their days by recounting the wonderful memories of their life. Remember that death is still a mystery, and you need not always have a solution. Allow them to feel and experience any fear they may have about what is to come. The key is to be there *unconditionally* when the fear comes up and they scream for a miracle. Your constant reassurance about the next phase of existence will help them to heal. After the initial denial and anger, eventually comes acceptance of where they are and where they are going.

Learn all you can about the afterlife, so that your own fears do not cause you to ignore their feelings about what is happening to them! This breeds isolation. Once they have reached acceptance, they will need to talk, and your silence will be invaluable, so listen with an open heart and mind. When they tell you about vivid dreams and visions of deceased loved ones and angels, don't dismiss them as ridiculous. Know that their consciousness straddles the veil, and they probably *are* having those visions.

The spirituality of impending death is of vital importance. Read to them stories of near-death experiences, the afterlife and post-death communication. Teach them about prayer. And the soothing practice of the "sound" meditation will bring the awareness necessary to complete the transition comfortably and without fear.

Avoid hollow statements such as, "It's God's will that this is happening." Instead, help them to understand that crossing the bridge is the most important event in their life and that they will pick up on the other side without missing a beat. Death is, indeed, a continuation of life and their soul has decided that it's time to take that step. This preparation will make for a peaceful, gentle passing.

If you happen to be present when it's time for them to leave the physical body, you can do several things to make it a tranquil experience. First, if there is no risk of contagion, do not be afraid to touch them, no matter how revolting they may look. There is *nothing* more therapeutic than the human touch, so hold their hand, massage their broken body, and embrace them with all your might. Pray with them, and guide them through the "sound" meditation. Even if they're in a coma, I assure you that they *can* hear you—I certainly could—even if they can't talk back. They're so thankful to have you there with them, so talk to them.

Please tell your readers and students to continue to pray for the deceased, before, during and after their transition. Remember, prayer is extremely powerful because it is composed of pure, intense loving thoughts. Such an outpouring of love from you really assists in letting us know we are not forgotten. Although the Divine Love we feel here fills in all the gaps, prayer makes the spirit brighter and more joyful so that we are better able to move forward in our own progression.

Finally, give them permission to let go. If you concentrate hard enough, you will actually sense and experience their passing with them. Tell them you are with them and not to be afraid. Gentle, relaxing words will direct them into the light. And as they take their last breath, send them as many loving thoughts as you can. For this is the fuel they will need for the next step of the journey.

Q. How can we best prepare for our own transition?

A. The best way to begin to prepare for your own passing is to live according to the two most important tenets in the universe—love and service. It matters not the amount of earthly goods you have acquired or what your social status is, for during your life review, you will be asked, "What have you done for your fellow man?"

Your answer will determine the level of consciousness to which you will "vibrate" and how peaceful your first stage of the afterlife will be. Your answer will also decide how "advanced" your new existence will be. You see, the more situations you master during your physical life, the more intense your progression when you enter this new existence.

An understanding of the nature of the afterlife helps dissipate the fear that often accompanies the onset of death, so my advice is to read, read, read. Study the many resources available to assist you on this journey. It is a sad fact that Western culture does not teach the spirituality necessary for a peaceful transition, so equipping yourself with the truth, and practicing it, falls to you.

Meditation is an excellent preparation. During the sound meditation described earlier, the sound you will hear is your own distinct tone, and is exactly what you will hear as you make your transition. This sound pattern will carry you into the next stage of consciousness, and if you are familiar with it and know what to expect, you will not encounter any resistance or fear.

Q. What impact does people's grief have on the one making the transition? Any advice to those suffering from excessive grief?

A. As we begin to make the transition, we find ourselves frustrated with your grief. We want to reassure you that we're okay and have just "gone into the next room." If you're worried about our pain immediately before death, you should know that most of the time, we never feel a thing. In the case of terminal illness, during the last stages of life, the spirit goes in and out of the body, and during the "out" periods, we feel no physical pain. In the case of accident, know that the spirit usually exits the body moments before any bodily trauma ever occurs.

Getting back to the subject of grief, most of us still have earthly emotions during this first stage, and although they're not as intense as when we were in our bodies, we still resonate with your grief. However, our guides are with us, gently helping us through it and encouraging us to the next step. For you see, our journey onward to new heights of awareness is a vital part of our growth here on this side. Prolonged sadness and "unhealthy" grief on your part may prevent us from going on.

Grief is necessary for those left behind, and we are coached on the stages of grief you must go through in order to heal. As you discovered, Walda, your spiritual foundation allowed you to process your grief, otherwise the wound would never have closed. We worry about you when your grief becomes unhealthy and threatens to hold you from your purpose and us from ours.

Instead of protracted grieving, we need your love and faith to carry us to a higher level. Detachment does not mean forgetting us, for we know that love is eternal and our connection can never be severed. But there is a difference between holding on and hanging on. Remember, we know that accepting that your loved one is no longer physically with you does not mean that you've forgotten about them.

For those who suffer from excessive grief, we suggest you start your healing by committing yourself to a whole new awareness. Open yourself to spirituality through prayer and meditation to open your heart, which will bring you to accept who you are in terms of what's happened. This new spirituality will help to dispel your suffering and loneliness. And because prayer and meditation are rooted in the heart, they will help to maintain the realization and love of the Source.

Keep an open mind about after-death communication and establish your own everlasting "connection," be it through active meditation or some other method. Spiritual awareness renews the faith so often lost in the struggle with grief and will allow you to live once more, fully and in peace.

Q. Connecting with you was difficult at first, but now it's no more difficult than crossing a bridge or entering another room. Most readers will have someone on the other side, and will be comforted to know that they are very much alive and are waiting to open a dialogue as we have done. So how can readers connect with their deceased loved ones?

A. We have talked about the many ways spirit communicates with you— dreams, visions, signs, and so on. Anything beyond that, such as connecting on a higher level of consciousness, has traditionally been reserved for the so-called "gifted" psychic medium. My dear readers, you are all *gifted psychic mediums!* You need only redevelop this skill, for it has been lying dormant since the day you started receiving societal programming to the contrary! Only three things are necessary to do this work: Desire, faith and patience. If you have all three, you *will* make contact on a most profound level. My wife has worked with many that are anxious to make the connection but few hold all three of these components. So let's talk about each one.

First, let's look at *desire*. How much do you *really* want to do this? Spirit communication is not a game or a parlor trick, and you must be totally dedicated to it once you begin. Desire comes from a place in the heart and brings with it the love needed to cross the bridge to our world.

Your intentions are equally as important. If you're looking to spend most of your waking hours connecting with your loved one, the experience will not be productive. You need balance. It's possible to have regular contact with the other side while remaining grounded and centered in your own world. Moderation is the key.

If you have not yet accepted who you are in relation to the loss of your loved one, you're not ready to do this. You must have a clear understanding concerning your purpose here. If you still view death as frightening and confusing, you're not ready. As I said before, this is not a parlor game like the Ouija Board, and should be approached only with the highest and best intention for you and those on the other side.

However, if you want to be close to our world and you understand what death really is, you are indeed ready to reconnect with your loved one, to gain wisdom and most importantly, to pass this enlightenment on to others.

Next, how is your *faith* these days? Have you mastered what faith really means? Are you absolutely *convinced* that you will make contact? If you answered no, again, you're not ready.

Fear is an obstacle to spirit communication, for fear is the absence of faith. If you're afraid of this process in any way, you're not ready. But if you really know what faith means, and have an unwavering belief that you will make contact, then you are ready.

The last component is *patience*. Wanting things to happen right away is a natural human trait because of the physical plane anxiety about never having enough time. Try to let go of the time issue, for it's not important over here. Understand that it may not happen right away. While you are probably ready to work toward this new awareness, practice is involved. Consistency is more important than intensity. As with learning any new skill, the more you practice, the faster you will become proficient. Intensity will come when you have mastered the process of connecting.

Here are some points that are necessary in understanding the process of spirit communication. We know that the brain and the mind are not the same. And we know that the brain does not survive death as does the consciousness of the mind. Your mind is extraordinary. It is both a transmitter and receiver. It is uniquely powerful and yet you tap only a fraction of its resources in daily life. But it is through the mind that you will cross the bridge from the physical world to the world of spirit. By raising the frequency of your consciousness through total relaxation of the body, meditation will gently guide you to the dimension where your loved one now lives.

If you do not already regularly practice meditation, your first seven days would best be spent learning to meditate, for it is with this knowledge that you will begin to see how the inner mind works. You will meet your Higher Self and discover the beauty and wisdom of the spiritual realms. Begin with fifteen minutes a day, and over time, the duration will naturally increase at its own pace. For now, concentrate on being *consistent*. You will be tempted to skip over this important first step but I urge you not to. If you jump ahead into trying to make contact without building the proper foundation, you will be discouraged with your results and will probably never attempt it again.

After you have completed your seven days of meditation practice, you are ready to begin one of the most exciting experiences of your life. Know that some sessions will be more intense than others, and it is important to approach this without expectation of outcome. Know that it will happen—that you will indeed make contact. But don't worry about the "when" or "how." Just let everything flow. Trust your spirit to guide you. Relax and enjoy the ride.

At some point, the question will arise, "Am I really in contact? Is this really spirit communication or just me talking to me? Am I really capable of such an awesome feat?"

When this happens, thank your ego for its healthy skepticism and let it go so that you can relax back into the process. When you truly believe that you can make contact, you will. And after a while, you will indeed *know* that you are truly connecting with your loved one.

How contact comes differs for different people. Some will *see*, others will *hear*, yet others will just *know*, as thoughts are dropped in the mind. So avoid any preformed expectations about how contact will come. Like a baby learning to see, initially things may be fuzzy, but over time, you will notice improvements in the clarity of what you see, hear, think or feel.

Imagination is the tool for making contact. For most of your life, you have been programmed to think that imagination means make-believe. It does not. When you "image" something in your mind, you are using imagination. The imagination is where all great ideas start and is the vehicle for your thoughts. Thoughts are energy and energy is very real. So detach from the make-believe aspect and let's move on.

Until you become comfortable with raising your frequency, your loved one will need to lower his or hers to make contact. This is not the most pleasant experience for us here because we are so used to our new "lightness." But we are patient because we see your dedication and know that you are still learning. I will tell you that your loved ones are have much to share and talk about, and they realize how much it will mean to you to be able to "feel" them once again.

Everyone I talk to here agrees that it's best to set aside a designated time every day to make contact. While linear time has no significance to us, it provides both dimensions with a structure of sorts, and in the beginning, until there is a total "blending" of consciousness, such a structure helps strengthen the contact.

Set aside a time of day when you will not be interrupted. You deserve this sacred time and you will soon find yourself looking forward to it. Turn off the phone and tell everyone you are going to be relaxing for the next fifteen minutes. Light some candles, preferably white. Burn incense or have scented flowers in the room. If you wish, play soft music or an environmental track of the sounds of nature such as a babbling brook or ocean waves.

Because the mind/body connection is so strong, how you feel physically will directly affect your results. If you're not feeling well, wait until whatever it is has passed. If you're "overcharged" with negative energy, take time to let go of all the tension, stress and anxiety. Stand up and "shake" it all off before you begin.

Next, settle comfortably into your favorite meditative position. Close your eyes and toss all negative thoughts out into the universe to be transformed into positive, loving energy. Say your prayer for protection.

When you're relaxed, focus on your heart chakra, the energy center in your chest, and your connection to divine love. Connection with your loved one will occur through the heart chakra, so breathe directly into it, and imagine beautiful white light filling up your chest area. Feel the warmth from this light open you to an awareness of peace. Continue breathing the white light into your chest area, feeling it bring you closer to your loved one.

Now, form a mental picture of your loved one in your mind's eye. Take your time and wait until you see them as clearly as possible. Look into their eyes and feel their presence. You will see them smile and wave "hello" and it is then that you will know that they are really with you. You have called to them and they have come.

Now, stay focused on your breathing and imagine the white light turning to a soft pink, the highest energy of love. Send this pink light out to your loved one, gently directing it toward their heart center. Feel its intensity build as the pink cord connects your heart centers in a most profound and penetrating way. Feel the love and peace that this connection brings and know that it's real. You have made contact.

Relax and enjoy each other's company. Take this time to share and to love once again. Pay attention to what's happening. Along with this telepathic exchange, you may also become aware of fragrant aromas and heavenly music. Don't try to analyze or doubt what takes place. Just enjoy it and let it flow from the universe. Know that you now have this new awareness of the spiritual realms and can return at any time.

When you're ready to say goodbye, tell your loved one when you propose to hold your next meeting. Watch as he or she smiles and waves "goodbye." Gently open your eyes. Take a deep breath and come back into the room. Feel your energy returning, feeling healthier and more joyful than ever before.

Postscript

As I finish the final draft of this writing, I am reminded again of how blessed my life has been. I took a step back and asked myself if I had it to do over again, what would I change? The answer came without hesitation: I wouldn't change a thing.

I have learned that there is no right or wrong way to live life. Every event provides an opportunity to gain wisdom. The intense sadness I have experienced has miraculously brought me closer to peace. I am now in a place of total trust and acceptance of who and where I am in the universal plan. And I have truly found my spiritual heritage. My sincere wish is to share this wisdom and love with all of you.

"When the student is ready, the teacher will appear."

— Walda Woods, September 3, 1999

Today is September 3, 1999, my new "birthday." Three earth years ago, I left my physical existence to return home to Spirit. My new world has given me many opportunities for growth and my progression continues in a most profound way. As these writings convey, my lovely wife and I made a soul promise to each other to do some very special work. Together, we hope to continue this mission of hope.

If I can leave you with some words of wisdom, they would be to live every day in total awareness. Practice love, compassion and forgiveness with everyone you meet, for they are all your teachers. Find your mission and work hard to help your soul experience what it is like to truly *BE*.

Please do not fear death for it is an inherent part of life. Your loved ones want you to know that they have not left you, and they continue to feel the love you once shared. When it is your turn to cross the bridge, they will take your hand and lead you into the light. And you will be home once again.

— Tom Woods, September 3, 1999

Annotated Reading List

Akehurst, Ken through G. M. Roberts. *Everyone's Guide To The Hereafter*. (Saffron Walden, Essex, United Kingdom: The C. W. Daniel Company Limited, 1985) This book was written through "automatic dictation" to prepare mankind for what awaits us on the other side.

Altea, Rosemary. *Proud Spirit*. (New York: Eagle Brook, 1997). This book offers a provocative glimpse into the spirit world and teaches that divine help is always available.

—— *The Eagle and the Rose*. (New York: Warner Books, 1995). The spiritual quest of a gifted clairvoyant.

Anderson, Joan Wester. *An Angel to Watch Over Me*. (New York: Ballentine Books, 1994). True stories of children's encounters with angels.

—— *Where Angels Walk*. (Sea Cliff, NY: Barton and Brett Publishing, 1992). True accounts of how angels have helped to transform and enhance the lives of many.

Atwater, P.M.H. *Beyond The Light*. (New York: Avon Books, 1994). After the author's near-death experience, she gives a most dynamic account of the world beyond.

Berman, Phillip L. *The Journey Home*. (New York: Pocket Books, 1996). A celebration of life, the healing power of love and the knowledge that death is not the end.

Bernard, Jan Selliken, R.N., N.D. and Miriam Schneider, R.N., C.R.N.H. *The True Work Of Dying*. (New York, NY: Avon Books, 1996) A practical and compassionate guide to easing the dying process for both the dying as well as their caretakers.

Brinkley, Dannion, and Paul Perry. *Saved By The Light*. (New York: HarperCollins, 1994). The author's amazing account of his near-death experience and how it transformed his views of life and death.

—— *At Peace In The Light*. (New York: HarperCollins, 1995). Dannion speaks about his newly acquired psychic abilities and the affects of his near-death experience.

Burnham, Sophy. *The Ecstatic Journey*. (New York: The Ballantine Publishing Group, 1997) The transforming power of mystical experience.

Chadwick, Gloria. *Discovering Your Past Lives*. (Chicago: Contemporary Books, 1988). Step-by-step program provides a clear explanation of karmic growth.

Chopra, Deepak. *Creating Affluence*. (New York: Amber Allen Publishing, 1993). Unlimited wealth is yours for the asking!

—— *The Seven Spiritual Laws of Success*. (New York: Amber Allen Publishing, 1993). Powerful principles that can easily be applied to create success in all areas of your life.

—— *The Way Of The Wizard*. (New York: Harmony Books, 1995). A quest for those who feel there is something important missing from their lives.

Cousineau, Phil. *Soul Moments*. (Berkeley, CA: Conari Press, 1997) Synchronicity and meaningful coincidences.

Cox-Chapman, Mally. *The Case for Heaven*. (New York: G.P. Putnam's Sons, 1995). Near-death experiences as evidence of life after death. An invaluable tool for the dying, their caregivers and families, and for the terminally ill.

Crawford, Jenny. *Through the Eyes of Spirit*. (Nevada City, California: Blue Dolphin Publishing, Inc., 1995). More evidence of life after death through this gifted medium. The grieving are consoled by her remarkable communications with the other side.

Currie, Ian. *You Cannot Die*. (Rockport, MA: Element Books, 1995). The incredible findings of a century of research on death.

Daniel, Alma, Timothy Wyllie and Andrew Ramer. *Ask Your Angels*. (New York: Ballantine Books, 1992). A guide to working with the messengers of heaven to empower and enrich your life.

Darling, David. *Soul Search*. (New York: Villard Books, 1995). A scientist breaks through the study of eternal awareness and presents some dynamic concepts on life, death and the afterlife.

Deaver, Korra, Ph.D. *Psychic Power And Soul Consciousness: The Metaphysics Of Personal Growth*. (Alameda, CA: Hunter House, Inc., 1991). Nine powerful workshops to increase psychic awareness and spiritual growth.

Devers, Edie, Ph.D. *Goodbye Again*. (Kansas City, MO: Andrews and McMeel, 1997). The author writes about her intense study into the field of ADC (After Death Communication). She has devoted her life's work to helping grieving patients come to terms with this phenomenon.

Dyer, Wayne. *Real Magic*. (New York, NY: HarperPaperbacks, 1992). The author teaches how to achieve a higher level of consciousness and offers specific strategies for attaining it.

—— *Manifest Your Destiny*. (New York, NY: Harper Collins Publishers, 1997). This gifted spiritual teacher offers nine principals for getting everything you want.

Eadie, Betty J. *Embraced By The Light*. (Placerville, CA: Gold Leaf Press, 1992). Called the most profound near-death experience ever, the author recounts the truths and realities she encountered and her new transformation.

Edward, John. *One Last Time*. (New York, NY: The Berkley Publishing Group, 1998). A psychic medium speaks to those we have loved and lost.

Fisher, Helen M. *From Erin With Love* (San Ramon, CA: Swallowtail Publishing, 1995. An inspiring story of hope and the continuation of life.

Foos-Graber, Anya. *Deathing*. (York Beach, ME: Nicolas-Hays, Inc., 1989) A step-by-step manual of meditations and exercises in preparation for death. An intelligent alternative for the final moments of life.

Georgian, Linda. *Communicating With the Dead*. (New York: Fireside, 1995). The author talks about bridging the communication gap between this world and the next. She provides comfort and hope to those who are grieving by letting them know that life goes on after we die.

Gonzalez-Wippler, Migene. *What Happens After Death?* (St. Paul, MN: Llewellyn Publications, 1997) Scientific and personal evidence for survival.

Griscom, Chris. *Time Is An Illusion*. (New York: Fireside Books, 1986). Spiritual healer and teacher shares insights gained by her enlightenment techniques.

Guggenheim, Bill and Judy Guggenheim. *Hello From Heaven!* (New York: Bantam Books, 1996). Firsthand accounts of after-death communications offer comfort, hope and inspiration.

Halberstam, Yitta and Judith Leventhal. *Small Miracles*. (Holbrook, MA: Adams Media Corporation, 1997) Extraordinary coincidences from everyday life.

Harpur, Tom. *Life After Death*. (Toronto, Ontario: McClelland & Stewart, Inc., 1991). The author researches evidence of life after death.

Hoffman, Enid. *Develop Your Psychic Skills*. (Atglen, PA: Whitford Press, 1981). Learn how to extend your awareness beyond your physical senses and to enhance the creativity and intuition that lies dormant within.

Jovanovic, Pierre. *An Inquiry Into The Existence Of Guardian Angels*. (New York: M. Evans and Company, Inc., 1995) A journalist's investigative report.

Kubler-Ross, Elisabeth, M.D. *The Wheel Of Life*. (New York, NY: Touchstone, 1997) The world famous thanatologist tells the story of her extraordinary life.

—— *Questions And Answers On Death And Dying*. (New York, NY: Touchstone, 1974) Answers to the most frequently asked questions about death.

Kubler-Ross, Elisabeth, M.D. *Death is of Vital Importance*. (Barrytown, NY: Station Hill Press, Inc., 1995). Once again, this gifted psychologist comes through with insights and understandings on how to care for the terminally ill.

—— *On Death and Dying*. (New York: Touchstone, 1997). A psychological study of death and dying brings hope to patients, their families and the professionals who care for them.

—— *On Life After Death*. (Berkley, CA: Celestial Arts, 1991). After many years of work with the dying, the author shares her feelings and opinions on this fascinating and controversial subject.

LaGrand, Louis E., Ph.D. *After Death Communication*. (St. Paul, MN: Llewellyn Publications, 1997) Extraordinary experiences of those mourning the death of loved ones.

LeShan, Lawrence, Ph. D. *The Medium, The Mystic And The Physicist*. (New York: Penguin Books, Inc., 1974) How mediums, mystics and physicists working toward a description of reality that is strikingly similar.

Levine, Stephen. *Who Dies?* (New York, NY: Doubleday, 1982) The author addresses the many aspects of dying with insight, candor and compassion. By far the most complete

manual on preparing for death and the grief that accompanies it.

Martin, Joel, and Patricia Romanowski. *Love Beyond Life*. (New York: HarperCollins Publishers, Inc., 1997). Based on years of research on bereavement and after death communications, the authors teach about the healing power of ADC and how to use it to attain comfort and peace when someone you love has died or is dying.

——— *We Are Not Forgotten: George Anderson's Messages Of Love And Hope From The Other Side.* (New York: Berkley Publishing, 1991). A collection of the psychic's most inspirational messages from the other side.

——— *We Don't Die: George Anderson's Conversations With The Other Side.* (New York: Berkley Publishing, 1988). The gifted psychic helps to heal the grieving and bereaved by contacting their loved ones in the next dimension.

——— *Our Children Forever. (New York: The Berkley Publishing Group, 1994). The psychic's remarkable messages from* children on the other side.

McCarty, Meladee, and Hanoch McCarty. *Acts Of Kindness: How To Create A Kindness Revolution.* (Deerfield Beach, FL: Health Communications, Inc., 1994). Thoughtful ways to make a difference in your everyday life.

Miller, Sukie, Ph.D. *After Death.* (New York, NY: Simon Schuster, 1997) New and challenging ways to reflect on the journey after death.

Millman, Dan. *The Life You Were Born To Live: A Guide To Finding Your Life Purpose.* (Tiburon, CA: H.J. Kramer, Inc., 1993). A modern method based on ancient wisdom to help you find new meaning, purpose and direction.

Mischell, Patricia. *Beyond Positive Thinking.* (Cincinnati, Ohio: Twin Lakes Publishing, 1993). By far the best book of its kind. This world famous parapsychologist offers specific "mind power" techniques for achieving physical and spiritual harmony and inner peace. [Patricia Mischell offers an extensive library of audio and video tapes, books and seminars on many psychic and spiritual topics, including a six cassette seminar on "What Happens When We Die". She is available for readings in spirit communications, past lives, personal readings, angel readings, animal readings and murder and missing persons cases. Please call her office in Cincinnati at 513-563-1744 for a list of materials, services and prices.]

Moen, Bruce. *Voyage Beyond Doubt* (Charlottesville, VA: Hampton Roads Publishing Company, 1998) From his Exploring the Afterlife series, the author discovers his deep faith through personal exploration of the afterlife.

Moen, Larry. *Meditations for Awakening.* (Naples, Florida: United States Publishing, 1994). The absolute best collection of guided imageries ever written. Utilizing visualization to improve physical and emotional health.

Montgomery, Ruth. *Companions Along The Way*. (New York: Ballantine Books, 1974). Revelations of previous incarnations of Ruth Montgomery, Edgar Cayce, Arthur Ford, Henry Kissinger and more.

—— *A World Beyond*. (New York: Ballantine Books, 1971). One of the world's most renowned psychics opens the door to the other side with ease and explains about life after death.

Moody, Raymond, Jr. M.D. *Life After Life*. (New York: Bantam Books, 1975). Astonishing research on the near-death experience—a chronicle of true accounts from death's survivors.

Morrissey, Dianne, Ph.D. *Anyone Can See The Light*. (Walpole, NH: Stillpoint Publishing, 1996). The seven keys to a guided out-of-body experience.

Morse, Melvin, M.D. with Paul Perry. *Closer to the Light*. (New York: Villard Books, 1990). This book chronicles experiences children report during near-death-experiences. Dr. Morse's scientific and analytical view of the phenomenon will convert even the most hardened skeptics.

—— *Parting Visions*. (New York: Villard Books, 1994) Uses and meanings of pre-death, psychic and spiritual experiences.

Murphy, Joseph. *The Amazing Laws of Cosmic Mind Power*. (West Nyack, NY: Parker Publishing, 1965). Combining the insights of world religion with the discoveries of modern psychology, a new level of spiritual understanding is introduced.

—— *The Power Of Your Subconscious Mind*. (Paramus, NJ: Prentice Hall, 1963) Combining ancient wisdom with modern science, this is one of the most powerful and widely read self-help books ever written.

Myss, Caroline, Ph.D. *Anatomy of the Spirit*. (New York: Harmony Books, 1996). A motivational breakthrough of mind, body and spiritual healing.

North, Anthony. *The Paranormal—A Guide To The Unexplained*. (London: Cassell PLC-Wellington House, 1996) A guide to the unexplained—life after death, mind over matter, time anomaly, astral travel, near death experience and more.

Northrop, Suzane. *The Seance*. (New York: Dell Publishing, 1994). A collection of the author's most interesting channeled group readings.

Novak, Peter. *Division Of Consciousness*. (Charlottesville, VA: Hampton Roads Publishing Co., Inc., 1997) A scientist's findings on the split consciousness, placing a whole new emphasis on the process of reincarnation.

Osis, Karlis, Ph.D and Erlendur Haraldsson, Ph.D. *At The Hour Of Death*. (Norwalk, CT: Hastings House, 1977) Doctors' and caregivers' accounts of events happening right before death occurs.

Perala, Robert and Tony Stubbs. *The Divine Blueprint: Roadmap for the New Millennium*. (Campbell, CA: United Light Publishing, 1998). The new millennium awaits, ascension is near and preparation is of utmost importance. The author shares the startling yet intelligent wisdom revealed to him by extraterrestrial emissaries.

——— *The Divine Architect: The Art of Living and Beyond*. (Campbell, CA: United Light Publishing, 2000). The account of the full cycle of life, from a soul's decision to reincarnate, coming to the earth plane, being here, and returning home. Includes a broad survey of types of after-death communication and spirit contacts through psychic mediums, including excerpts from *Conversations with Tom*.

Price, Jan. *The Other Side Of Death*. (New York: Ballantine Books, 1996). The author tells of her near-death experience and how it changed her view of death as well as life itself.

Puryear, Anne. *Steven Lives!* (New York: Pocket Books, 1992). The author's son, Steven, committed suicide at the age of 15. He began contacting her soon after with some startling yet inspirational messages that she shares in the hopes that they will bring healing to the loved ones of suicide victims.

Randles, Jenny and Peter Hough. *Life After Death & The World Beyond*. (New York, NY: Sterling Publishing Company, 1998). Leading paranormal researchers investigate the case for heaven.

Redfield, James. *The Celestine Prophecy*. (New York, NY: Warner Books, 1995). Wisdom from an ancient Peruvian manuscript that will guide your perceptions of why you are where you are in your life and direct you with new energy and optimism.

——— *The Tenth Insight*. (New York: Warner Books, 1996). Dynamic sequel to *The Celestine Prophecy*.

Ritchie, Jean. *Death's Door*. (New York: Dell Publishing, 1994). A collection of true near-death experiences, including those of children and celebrities. Also, some astonishing scientific research.

Roberts, J Aelwyn. *Yesterday's People*. Rockport, MA: Element Books, Inc., 1997). A parson's search for the answers to life after death.

Roger, John and Peter McWilliams. *We Give To Love*. (Los Angels, CA: Prelude Press, 1993). "If you were arrested for kindness, would there be enough evidence to convict you?" Notes and quotes on the joys of heart-felt service.

Roman, Sanaya, and Duane Packer. *Creating Money: Keys To Abundance*. (Tiburon, CA: H.J. Kramer, Inc., 1988). A guide to manifesting prosperity and success in abundance.

Sherwood, Keith. *The Art Of Spiritual Healing*. (St. Paul, MN: Llewellyn Publications, 1985). Learn how to tap the incredible healing power within you.

Steiner, Rudolf. *Life Beyond Death*. (London, England: Rudolf Steiner Press, 1995). Selected lectures by the author, whose research through clairvoyance has given mankind credible insight into what happens after physical death.

Steinpach, Dr. Richard. *Why We Live After Death*. (Gambier, OH: Grail Foundation Press, 1996) By applying the basic Laws of Nature, the author explains how we continue to develop after physical death.

Stern, Jess. Edgar Cayce: *The Sleeping Prophet*. (New York: Doubleday Books, 1967). The life, prophecies and readings of America's most famous mystic.

Stratton, Elizabeth, M. S. *Seeds Of Light*. (New York: Simon and Schuster, 1997). Healing meditations for body and soul.

Stubbs, Tony. *An Ascension Handbook*. (Lithia Springs, GA: New Leaf, 1999). Learn more about the end of karma and the reuniting with Spirit in this "how to" manual for ascension. Channeled through the Ascended Master Serapis, the material prepares the reader for the increasing frequencies of our energy bodies as we approach the new millenium.

Taylor, Terry Lynn. *Answers From The Angels*. (Tiburon, CA: H.J. Kramer, Inc., 1993). An inspirational collection of readers' letters relating their angel experiences.

—— *Guardians Of Hope*. (Tiburon, CA: H.J. Kramer, Inc., 1992). Sixty angel practices for making life work better.

—— *Messengers Of Light*. (Tiburon, CA: H.J. Kramer, Inc., 1990). A practical guide to including angels in your life.

Thurston, Mark, Ph.D. *Synchronicity As Spiritual Guidance*. (Virginia Beach, VA: A.R.E. Press, 1997). Using everyday coincidences and signs as a form of guidance. These resources come from the world around us as well as our inner lives.

Van Praagh, James. *Talking To Heaven*. (New York: Penguin Books, 1997). A medium's message of life after death.

Walsch, Neale Donald. *Conversations With God–Book 1* (New York: G.P. Putnam's Sons, 1996). The author connects with God and receives insightful answers to our most commonly asked questions.

—— *Conversations With God-Book 2* (Charlottesville, VA: Hampton Roads Publishing Company, Inc., 1997). The dialogue with God continues.

—— *Conversations With God-Book 3* (Charlottesville, VA: Hampton Roads Publishing Company, Inc., 1998). In the third and final book of his trilogy, the author's dialogue with God offers an abundance of eye-opening information.

Wiitala, Geri Colozzi. *Heather's Return*. (Virginia Beach, VA: A.R.E. Press, 1996). Spiritual signs from her deceased daughter leads the author's family on a journey of hope and renewed faith in God.

Wilber, Ken. *The Spectrum Of Consciousness*. (Wheaton, IL: The Theosophical Publishing House, 1993). A reference point for integrating psychology and spirituality.

Williamson, Linda. *Contacting The Spirit World*. (New York: Berkley Books, 1997) How to develop your psychic abilities and stay in touch with loved ones.

Williamson, Marianne. *A Return To Love*. (New York: HarperCollins, 1992). Based on the teachings of A Course In Miracles, the book covers the practice of love as a daily answer to the problems that confront us.

Wilson, Ian. *The After Death Experience*. (New York, NY: Willaim Morrow and Company, Inc., 1987). Insightful evidence from a variety of sources explores the world of the unknown and the continuation of life.

Young-Sowers, Meredith. *Agartha: A Journey To The Stars*. (Walpole, NH: Stillpoint Publishing, 1995). A gentle yet intense journey into awareness, told by the author through her spiritual guide, Mentor.

Zukav, Gary. *The Seat Of The Soul*. (New York: Fireside Books, 1990). A dynamic teaching of thought, evolution and journey of the spirit.

Notes

[1] Quite by "accident," I have since found this book: *Deathing* by Anya Foos-Graber. Her remarkable "deathing" techniques will enrich the lives of many.

[2] I was amazed at this new perspective on reincarnation, and since this dictation, I have found other references to this philosophy. Joel Martin and Patricia Romanowski's book titled *Love Beyond Life* contains comparable information by Dr. Jong Ree, an oriental acupuncturist. *The Division Of Consciousness* by Peter Novak concludes that there are two parts of the psyche, the conscious and the unconscious, and names these as the soul and the spirit. A fascinating theory on reincarnation ensues and is strikingly similar to Tom's explanation.

[3] Not long after Tom dictated this meditation, I found a similar exercise in the book *Deathing* by Anya Foos-Graber. Apparently, it's an ancient yogamudra technique used exclusively for enlightenment in the fundamentals of yoga. .

[4] Matthew 21:22

[5] Mark 11:24

[6] The spiritual, emotional and mental bodies are "anchored" to the physical body by seven energy centers called "chakras," the Sanskrit word for "wheel," so named because of their shape. The center most involved in processing the energy of love is the one in the center of the chest, called the heart chakra. Tom returns to this topic in more depth later.

About the Authors

Walda Woods attended Merrimack College in Massachusetts where she completed a course of study in Business Management. Her interest in business eventually led her to become a successful real estate broker in 1985. She has since climbed the corporate ladder to become Director of Sales for IDG World Expo in 1993. In 1995 she began her own consulting firm, offering Sales Planning and Development services to a variety of businesses.

On September 3, 1996, life dealt her a most tragic blow—the loss of her husband and best friend, Tom. Tom, a healthy, athletic, non-smoker, loved life with a passion. Never sick a day in his 45 years, he died suddenly from a massive heart attack during a neighborhood Labor Day cookout. The grief that Walda experienced at his passing led her through a maze of emotions, ranging from anger, denial and depression. However, her deep faith and the often intense communication with Tom has helped her maintain a balance in her life and allowed her to heal.

Walda's hobby of writing poetry and short stories since 1972 allowed her to express herself and hone her skills as a writer, skills she now used to tell her intimate story of loss, grief, and healing in *Conversations With Tom: An Adventure in After-death Communication*. Guided by the spirit of her late husband, Tom, she refers to this labor of love as "one woman's spiritual journey through grief." Her message to readers is two-fold: no one ever really dies; and love is the ultimate connecting energy between this world and the next.

Walda is currently enrolled in a course of study in metaphysics and thanatology at Northern Essex Community College in Massachusetts as well as at The Mastermind Seminars School of Psychic Study through world famous parapsychologist Patricia Mischell in Cincinatti, Ohio.

Walda volunteers at the Lazarus House Ministries (a local homeless shelter), for various civic organizations, the local Hospice Association, and the Trauma Intervention Program. She currently leads workshops and support groups in spiritual grief recovery. She is also a member of the Association for Death Education and Counseling and conducts lectures on the subjects of death, dying and the afterlife.

She resides in North Andover, Massachusetts with her cats, Ben and Jerry. She can be reached via e-mail at Noel95@aol.com.